About This Book

"*Indian Spirit* is a very beautiful book combining excellent photos with fine and meaningful quotations from the most prominent Plains Indians in the last one hundred and fifty years. Recommended reading for anyone who is interested in American history. The editor, Michael Fitzgerald, has managed with great consideration and understanding to compose this invaluable book."

—**Åke Hultkrantz**, author of *Religions of the American Indians* and *Native Religions of North America: The Power of Visions and Fertility*

"One can get lost in contemplating these photographed faces, the weathered skin of natural men, the dignity which is the outward manifestation of inner strength, patience, and wisdom. These men were leaders by dint of their depth of character.… As for the quotations: simple grandeur from those who lived on the very face of the earth and the edge of existence."

—**James Alexander Thom**, author of *Follow the River*, *The Long Knife*, and *The Red Heart*

"No other book on my desk has so keenly caught the attention and personal interest of my students as much as Michael Oren Fitzgerald's *Indian Spirit*. This revealing compilation of striking portraiture wed with the words of prominent Native Americans speaks with great clarity and grace of their truly unique and reverent worldview. This work has inspired intense, thought provoking student discourse—so much so that I plan to include it among the required religious texts in my Intellectual Heritage class."

—**Gerald Musinsky**, Temple University

"It is impossible not to be deeply moved when turning the pages of this beautiful book. The pictures and texts were carefully selected to convey the deepest dimension of the Indian spirit. The texts illuminate American Indian spirituality while correcting common misinterpretations. The selection of Native American portraits, some well known and others presented for the first time in such a setting, puts the reader face to face with what the Native American spirit is all about: dignity, nobility of bearing, straightforwardness, domination of self, discipline of gesture, courage, a deep combination of power and peace, and a sense of the sacred."

—**Jean-Pierre Lafouge**, Marquette University

"*Indian Spirit* is a wonderful book, containing not only beautiful photographs of Native Americans but also significant examples of their eloquent words of wisdom. Michael O. Fitzgerald and World Wisdon, Inc. are to be commended for this inspiring publication."

—**Raymond Wilson**, Fort Hays State University

"This little book is a gem. It offers wonderful insights into the mind and heart of the American Indian. No genuine ecologist can afford to ignore its message. Regardless of one's own spiritual roots, the wisdom of these 'Medicine men' is powerfully enlightening."

—**Rama Coomaraswamy**, author of *The Invocation of the Name of Jesus: As Practiced in the Western Church and The Destruction of the Christian Tradition*

"*Indian Spirit* is unusually handsome, the quality of the portraits outstanding. They are old friends, but reproduced more beautifully than ever in this volume. Congratulations."

—**Father Peter J. Powell**, Director, Saint Augustine's Center for American Indians, author of *Sweet Medicine*

World Wisdom
The Library of Perennial Philosophy

The Library of Perennial Philosophy is dedicated to the exposition of the timeless Truth underlying the diverse religions. This Truth, often referred to as the *Sophia Perennis*—or Perennial Wisdom—finds its expression in the revealed Scriptures as well as the writings of the great sages and the artistic creations of the traditional worlds.

Indian Spirit: Revised and Enlarged appears as one of our selections in the Sacred Worlds series.

Sacred Worlds Series

The Sacred Worlds series blends images of visual beauty with focused selections from the writings of the great religions of the world, including both scripture and the writings of the sages and saints. Books in the Sacred Worlds series may be based upon a particular religious tradition, or upon a universal religious theme such as prayer or virtue.

Praise for the Sacred Worlds Series

"[This series] combines impressive imagery—both new and old fine arts, as well as contemporary and vintage photography—with selections from world faith traditions.... These entries in the 'Sacred Worlds' series are delights to the eye and the mind."

—Library Journal

World Wisdom's Other American Indian Titles

All Our Relatives: Traditional Native American Thoughts about Nature
compiled and illustrated by Paul Goble, 2005

The Feathered Sun: Plains Indians in Art and Philosophy
by Frithjof Schuon, 1990

The Gospel of the Redman: Commemorative Edition
compiled by Ernest Thompson Seton and Julia M. Seton, 2005

Indian Spirit
edited by Michael Oren Fitzgerald, 2003

Light on the Indian World:
The Essential Writings of Charles Eastman (Ohiyesa)
edited by Michael Oren Fitzgerald, 2002

Native Spirit: The Sun Dance Way
edited by Michael Oren Fitzgerald, 2007

The Spirit of Indian Women
edited by Judith Fitzgerald and Michael Oren Fitzgerald, 2005

The Spiritual Legacy of the American Indian:
Commemorative Edition
by Joseph Epes Brown, 2007

Tipi: Home of the Nomadic Buffalo Hunters
compiled and illustrated by Paul Goble, 2007

Films about American Indian Spirituality by World Wisdom

Native Spirit: The Sun Dance Way, 2007

Indian Spirit
Revised and Enlarged

Edited by

Michael Oren Fitzgerald
& Judith Fitzgerald

Introduction by

Thomas Yellowtail

Foreword by
James Trosper

www.worldwisdom.com

Indian Spirit:
Revised and Enlarged
©2006 World Wisdom, Inc.

Design by Judith Fitzgerald

Library of Congress Cataloging-in-Publication Data

Indian spirit / edited by Michael Oren Fitzgerald & Judith Fitzgerald ; intro-
duction by Thomas Yellowtail ; foreword by James Trosper. – Rev. and enl.
    p. cm. – (Sacred worlds series)
  Includes bibliographical references and index.
  ISBN-13: 978-1-933316-19-2 (pbk. : alk. paper)
  ISBN-10: 1-933316-19-5 (pbk. : alk. paper) 1. Indians of North America-
-Portraits. 2. Indian philosophy–North America. I. Fitzgerald, Michael
Oren, 1949- II. Fitzgerald, Judith, 1951- III. Series: Sacred worlds series
(Bloomington, Ind.)
  E89.I62 2006
  973.04'97–dc22

                                                            2006016150

Printed on acid-free paper in China.

For information address World Wisdom, Inc.
P.O. Box 2682, Bloomington, Indiana 47402-2682

www.worldwisdom.com

Table of Contents

Dedication

This book is dedicated to all American Indians.
May they perpetuate the essential qualities of their ancestors.

All of the royalties from this book are being donated to the Smithsonian's
Museum of the American Indian, in the hope that this museum will help
preserve the Indian spirit for future generations.

Preface

How can a person of the 21st century understand the essential character of the nomadic American Indians of the 19th century? What lessons can we learn from the Native Americans about God's immeasurable, wild, and virgin Nature? Is there a way to learn the spiritual wisdom of the olden-day Indians directly from the source? While the nomads of the plains and forests have long since vanished, we can still glimpse the spirit of that irreplaceable world directly through the words and photographs of the warriors and sages that have been preserved to our day. This book is an elegy for those great chiefs, who are the paragons of Plains Indian life. It is meant to communicate their wisdom and their beauty of soul, expressed so eloquently and poignantly by their own words and their own faces. While all of the American Indians presented here have long since passed from this earth, the heroic ideal that they represent, blending the qualities of the priest and the warrior stands as a model for all people.[1]

Many of these photographs have never before been published, so how have they been selected? Most of the photographs in this selection are taken from several thousand photographs that we have collected over the past thirty years. The majority of the photos in our collection are the result of research done in the Library of Congress in 1974.[2] All of the photographs ever submitted for copyright protection are in that facility, and at that time it was still possible to roam freely through the stacks and to easily obtain copies of

1. *Indian Spirit* contains wisdom from many American Indian tribes, but it has a certain focus on the Plains Indians because they were the last group of tribes to succumb to the white encroachment and thus their wisdom and their photographs are the best preserved of all American Indian tribes. When considering Plains Indian spirituality, it is evident that the many variations among the tribes are too vast and diverse to create a definitive statement about what it entails; but few would deny that there are unifying themes, including the sacred quality of virgin Nature, the Directions of Space, the use of the Sacred Pipe, and above all the idea of a Supreme Being. This book focuses on those common themes. While Indian women expressed a complementary perfection, no women have been included because they are the focus of a companion volume: *The Spirit of Indian Women* (cited in the Appendix). As with other civilizations, it is evident that not all American Indians lived up to the cultural ideal, but that ideal is nevertheless a reality.

2. The photograph of Black Elk on page 20 was taken by the late Joseph Epes Brown in 1947 and is used with the kind permission of his family. Dr. Brown was a professor of Religious Studies at the University of Montana and a well-known authority on the Plains Indians.

those photographs whose copyright protection had expired. We limited our selection of photographs to men who were raised into manhood during the nomadic days of the Plains Indians prior to the reservation era.[3]

We are also grateful to include photographs from the collection of the late philosopher Frithjof Schuon, compiled by him over a period of some fifty years. Although well known among scholars of comparative religion, many readers will not be familiar with Schuon. From his youth, Schuon had a profound and ultimately lifelong interest in and affinity with the Plains Indians of North America. He was formally adopted into the family of Chief James Red Cloud,[4] a grandson of the great Sioux chief well known to history. Years later, he was adopted into the family of Thomas Yellowtail, the Crow Indian medicine man and Sun Dance chief, who was one of the most admired American Indian spiritual leaders of the last century,[5] and whose family is also one of the most famous American Indian families of the last century.[6] In a career that spanned more than 50 years, Schuon wrote over 25 books that touched on diverse aspects of all the world's great religions, including that of the Plains Indians. He corresponded with many American Indian leaders and received photographs from many sources. For example, the photograph of Black Elk, the renowned Sioux holy man, on page 21, was a gift from Black Elk and is inscribed "*Mita Kola, Hehaka Sapa*" [(to) my friend, (from) Black Elk].[7] For several of the photos in the Schuon collection, the identity of both chief and photographer are unknown,[8] as they were gifts to Schuon and the information was not provided to him.[9]

3. Photographic technology was not widely available until the second part of the 19th century, so there are few records of the nomadic tribes of the Eastern part of the United States. We have therefore only chosen photographs of the Western tribes, who still lived in virgin Nature during the first years of photography.

4. In 1959 at Pine Ridge, South Dakota, Chief James Red Cloud gave Schuon the Sioux name Brave Eagle, *Wambli Ohitika*. Some of the photographs in this book were gifts from James Red Cloud to Schuon.

5. The story of Yellowtail's life is revealed in *Yellowtail: Crow Medicine Man and Sun Dance Chief* (cited in the Primary Bibliography). For more information on Thomas Yellowtail, see "About Thomas Yellowtail" in the Appendix.

6. For information on the Yellowtail family, see "About Thomas Yellowtail" in the Appendix.

7. The handwriting is reproduced in actual size on page 21. It is not known whether this is Black Elk's handwriting or the handwriting of one of his relatives.

8. We are very grateful to Mike Cowdrey, one of the foremost experts on Native American photography, who painstakingly reviewed our manuscript and provided us with many missing names. Cowdrey corrected several errors in the recorded names of the men who appear on these pages.

9. In 1992, in response to our request, Frithjof Schuon reviewed both his photographic collec-

INDIAN SPIRIT

Our research on American Indian oratory and writings started in 1970 when Michael was the graduate teaching assistant for the course "Religious Traditions of the North American Indians" at Indiana University, taught by Joseph Epes Brown. It was through Dr. Brown that we met both Thomas and Susie Yellowtail and Benjamin Black Elk, the son of the revered Sioux holy man. From that time we have studied the American Indians, particularly the Plains Indians, continuously seeking out the oratory and writings that concerned the spiritual traditions of the pre-reservation nomads.

+‑+‑+

The traditional world of the American Indians had no written language, so written documentation of this wisdom starts with the coming of the white man. This greatly limits the overall time period for the direct recording of the words of the nomadic chiefs. As *Indian Spirit* only focuses on their sacred heritage, we have not included statements about the interaction with the dominant white culture unless there is a comparison of the sacred or moral values of the two races. In addition to the words of the great olden-day chiefs, we have added selected writings from the generation who was taught directly by these traditional nomads. All of the education of the young was through the oral teaching of the elders. This storytelling was the basis of the transmittal of the tribal wisdom from one generation to the next, or more precisely, from the generation of the grandparents to the grandchildren, because the children spent countless hours under the tutelage of the grandparents while the parents provided for the material needs of the family. This process was an integral part of the children's education and in this way each third generation provided a vital link to the ancestral tribal traditions. Plains Indian youth born around the turn of the 19th century still had the benefit of an integral education directly from the "old-timers," as many American Indians affectionately refer to the last generation that lived in the nomadic era of the Plains Indian culture. That generation was the last direct living link to the nomadic pre-reservation era, and most of them are no longer with us. While

tion and ours and identified many of the photographs that form the basis of this selection. We are grateful to him for his guidance and for allowing us to use several of his photographs and his sketches (pp. 10, 26, 50, 66, 90, 125, 130).

there is not a precise time that defines this generation, we have chosen only to include writings or oratory from the elders born before 1904.[10] Some of the quotations may be familiar, but some lesser known quotations have been included to demonstrate the breadth and diversity of tribal wisdom.

+‡+

The Introduction is the result of our relationship with the Yellowtail family, which began in 1970. Prior to Thomas Yellowtail's death in November 1993, we spent a part of every summer with him in the West, including annual visits to the Sun Dance. Beginning in 1978, Yellowtail also made annual trips to visit our home in Indiana. During this time together, we tried to work on various projects of interest to him, including the preparation of the Yellowtail book and then this book. He loved to see all of the photographs and read the writings and oratory of the old-timers that we found during the course of each passing year. Yellowtail finished the Introduction[11] while staying in our home in the autumn of 1992, after reviewing all of these photographs and quotations.[12] Though personal and professional obligations delayed the book's publication for several years, there is a sense of fulfillment now in completing what we worked on together.

10. This does not deny that much of the wisdom of these old-timers has been preserved in later generations, but the later generations did not have the benefit of learning directly from those who actually lived the traditional life of complete freedom in virgin Nature. The further one travels from the source, the more difficult it is to know the authenticity of the recorded words, owing to a wide variety of factors. We have tried to select writings that stay as close as possible to the source of the ancestral wisdom.

11. The process that Yellowtail used to write the Introduction is the same process that was utilized in recording and editing the Yellowtail book. In brief, we recorded his thoughts about the subject at hand, which we then edited and set onto paper, always trying to preserve his actual word choice and manner of speaking. He reviewed our drafts and made corrections, which we incorporated into a subsequent document. He always read and approved the final writing. We started this process in 1991 and completed the Introduction in 1992.

12. Since that time, Raymond Wilson, a professor at Fort Hays State University and the leading authority on the life of Ohiyesa (Charles Eastman), led us to the photographs of Ohiyesa on pages 12 and 13, which are provided courtesy of the Walter P. Reuther Library, Wayne State University. We also added selected quotations from the Yellowtail book. In all other respects, Yellowtail reviewed all of the photographs and the words of the chiefs at the time the Introduction was written. For diverse reasons, it was not possible to utilize all of the photographs and quotations that Yellowtail reviewed.

INDIAN SPIRIT

Indian Spirit introduces us to the foremost members of that tradition, in both photographs and words. We see the great emphasis the American Indians placed on moral character and their intimate contact with God's immeasurable, wild, and virgin Nature. It is evident that they strongly believe the sacred spirit within each person is mysteriously linked to the Great Spirit and that man's vocation is to live in harmony with the teachings of the Great Spirit. Their entire culture was built upon these precepts. In today's technological world, we often lose our connection to anything of sacred value that can provide a balance for the disequilibriating factors which we encounter on a daily basis. It is our hope that the insights conveyed in *Indian Spirit* will help each of us to better understand the sacred spirit that dwells in every person.

Judith and Michael Fitzgerald
May, 2006
Bloomington, Indiana

Foreword

Indian Spirit preserves the wisdom of our Elders for today's generation, and future generations. The words and images collected in this book will connect readers to the history of our native peoples and to the sacred ways given to us by the Creator.

Many tribes are represented here, from the Plains, Mountains, Coastal, Southwest, and other parts of North America. History divides the tribes of these vast geographic and cultural regions into friends, enemies, and strangers to each other. The life-ways of each people varied, but what *Indian Spirit* shows is that each of these ways is *good* because each was given to the people by the same Creator.

It is this connection to the Creator that gave Indian people their sacred center. Society today, Indian and non-Indian, has lost its sacred center. But our connection to the Creator can never be broken. As long as we wish to follow His ways, He will have pity on us, and bless us with the guidance we need to live a truly happy and spiritual life.

Indian Spirit offers a glimpse into the world of our ancestors. It shares with us their philosophies and deeply religious lives rooted in the teachings of the Creator. This sacred knowledge was revealed to our ancestors after much fasting and prayer. I pray that this book will be an inspiration to our youth and lead them back to the Red Road, which in turn will lead to the Creator. I also pray that this book will touch your heart.

James Trosper
Shoshone Sun Dance Chief
Trustee of the University of Wyoming

Introduction

I should start by raising my voice in a prayer.

Acbadadea, Maker of All Things Above, hear my prayer. Thank you for giving me the strength to help my people so that the Sun Dance Religion may carry on. I am retired now from being the Crow Sun Dance chief, but You have helped me to select a man to continue this sacred tradition. You have also allowed me to continue to have the strength to be a medicine man and I intend to continue to try to help others by my actions and by my words. I hope in this manner to help people see that they need to find a way that will lead to You.

You have given different ways to different people all over the world. As we know, this earth is round like a wagon wheel. In a wagon wheel, all the spokes are set into the center. The circle of the wheel is round and all spokes come from the center and the center is You, *Acbadadea,* the Maker of All Things Above. Each spoke can be considered as a different religion of the world which has been given by You to different people and different races. All of the people of the world are on the rim of the wheel and they must follow one of the spokes to the center. The different paths have been given to us but they all lead to the same place. We all pray to the same God, to You. There are different places on the wheel so each way may look strange to someone following a different path. It is easy for people to say that their way is the best if they know all about their faith and it is good for them. But they should refrain from saying bad things about other ways that they don't know about. There should be no hard feelings about someone else if he is following a way that leads to You. Help us to see this wisdom.

It is the responsibility of each person to choose a path and to pray. It does not matter which path they choose, as long as they follow some religion. It helps to understand the sacred way of other people in order to better understand your own religion. So I hope that this book will help the people who read it to remember their responsibility to live in a sacred manner by better understanding the spirit of the olden-day Indians.

I have read the words of the olden-day Indians that have been selected by my son, Michael Fitzgerald, and I have looked at the images that have been gathered together by my son [Michael] and my close friend, Frithjof Schuon. I am thankful that others may see these things, so that they may better understand the path that You have given to the Indians. *Aho*!

People will want to know how I met Frithjof Schuon. We first met in 1953 in Paris. In that summer of long ago, my wife and I were members of a group of Crow Indian dancers who toured Europe, North Africa, and the Middle East performing traditional Indian dances. In both 1959 and 1963 the Schuons traveled from Switzerland to the United States to attend the Sun Dance with me and to meet with Indians of many tribes. I was with Mr. Schuon in Sheridan, Wyoming in 1959 when he was adopted into the Sioux tribe in a ceremony at the All American Indian Days. Since he moved to America in 1980, we have come together each year for a visit. In 1987, I held a ceremony and adopted him as a member of my family. It is better that he is now both a Crow and a Sioux.

The idea for this book came from my son, Michael Fitzgerald, who has been a member of my family and the Crow tribe for over twenty years. He and his family come and attend the Crow Sun Dance every year and I stay with him each year in Bloomington, Indiana. Michael also had the idea to make a book about my life and the Crow Sun Dance, which was recently published.[1] In that book Michael helped to preserve the spiritual tradition of the Crow Sun Dance. Now Michael has helped to show us the wisdom of the old-timers with some of their best words. Because Michael and Mr. Schuon know and love the spirit of the Indians they have been able to find and select the best images of the old-timers that have ever been gathered together. *Aho*!

Our Medicine Fathers have given us two main plant medicines to use in our healing ceremonies. These plants only grow in one place in the world, and that is over at a certain place on the Shoshone reservation. This sacred location is guarded by two eagles, one a bald eagle and the other one a golden

---

1. Michael Fitzgerald, *Yellowtail: Crow Medicine Man and Sun Dance Chief*. See "Primary Bibliography" for more details.

Thomas Yellowtail
Crow Medicine Man
and Sun Dance Chief

eagle. Each time we go there to collect the medicine we say prayers, and in our prayers we always say a few words just for these two eagles, to thank them for protecting the sacred medicine. Years ago, when I adopted Michael as my son, I gave him the Crow name "Two Eagles," after these two eagles. So his name really means "Protects the Sacred Medicine." Michael is trying to live up to his name. This is very good.

INDIAN SPIRIT

This book makes me remember the times in my youth when all of the old-timers were living still. I can remember the fear and the admiration I felt when I was in their presence. I recall one of the chiefs in this book very well, because Chief Medicine Crow gave me my traditional name when I was growing up. He named me "Medicine Rock Chief" and I have spent my life trying to become worthy of such a name. There are many other chiefs that I remember and it is sad to know that as these people died, much of the sacred center of our traditional ways was lost with them. But what we have left is still good enough and if a person is able to pray and be sincere, then they will find their way to their Maker and this is good.

Words alone are inadequate to express spiritual realities. This book expresses the Indian spirit because it combines the best photographs ever taken of old-time chiefs with some of their best words. You can meet these old-timers and share their wisdom. People who read this book will better understand our sacred ways. *Aho*!

October, 1992
Bloomington, Indiana

May the great spirit keep watch over you and protect you always.

Tom Yellowtail

In the life of the Indian there was only one inevitable duty—the duty of prayer—the daily recognition of the Unseen and Eternal. His daily devotions were more necessary to him than daily food. He wakes at daybreak, puts on his moccasins, and steps down to the water's edge. Here he throws handfuls of clear, cold water into his face, or plunges in bodily. After the bath, he stands erect before the advancing dawn, facing the sun as it dances upon the horizon, and offers his unspoken orison. His mate may precede or follow him in his devotions, but never accompanies him. Each soul must meet the morning sun, the new sweet earth, and the Great Silence alone!

Ohiyesa (Charles Eastman)
Wahpeton Dakota

Facing the Sun

Medicine Crow
Absaroke

INDIAN SPIRIT

Medicine
Crow

<u>Wakan</u> <u>Tanka</u>
When I pray to Him
He hears me.
Whatever is good
He grants me.

Teton Sioux Song

When a person is on a vision quest, he must have certain attitudes and intentions for his prayers to be sincere, and then he must carry these over into his daily life. It is easy to forget what you learned during this trial; unless you remember to carry on your prayer continually during every day of your life, you will not have learned one of the most important purposes of the vision quest. Each time we talk about one of our sacred rites, you will hear me talk about the spiritual attitudes which a person must possess as that person participates in any rite. It is possible to learn the outer steps that must be accomplished in a rite without learning the inner meanings that are the keys to the sacred traditions. Each seeker must therefore open his heart to the Great Mystery as he tries to follow the sacred way, because the perfect accomplishment of the outer steps of a rite will be worth nothing without the knowledge of the inner meanings.

Yellowtail, Absaroke

Medicine Crow

Revenger
Absaroke

INDIAN SPIRIT

I am blind and do not see the things of this world; but when the Light comes from Above, it enlightens my heart and I can see, for the Eye of my heart sees everything. The heart is a sanctuary at the center of which there is a little space, wherein the Great Spirit dwells, and this is the Eye. This is the Eye of the Great Spirit by which He sees all things and through which we see Him. If the heart is not pure, the Great Spirit cannot be seen, and if you should die in this ignorance, your soul cannot return immediately to the Great Spirit, but it must be purified by wandering about in the world. In order to know the center of the heart where the Great Spirit dwells you must be pure and good, and live in the manner that the Great Spirit has taught us. The man who is thus pure contains the Universe in the pocket of his heart.

Black Elk
Oglala Lakota

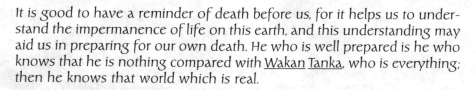

It is good to have a reminder of death before us, for it helps us to understand the impermanence of life on this earth, and this understanding may aid us in preparing for our own death. He who is well prepared is he who knows that he is nothing compared with <u>Wakan</u> <u>Tanka</u>, who is everything; then he knows that world which is real.

Black Elk

Two Guns
Blackfeet

INDIAN SPIRIT

We saw the Great Spirit's work in almost everything: sun, moon, trees, wind, and mountains. Sometimes we approached Him through these things. Was that so bad? I think we have a true belief in the supreme being, a stronger faith than that of most whites who have called us pagans.... Indians living close to nature and nature's ruler are not living in darkness.

Did you know that trees talk? Well they do. They talk to each other, and they'll talk to you if you listen. Trouble is, white people don't listen. They never learned to listen to the Indians so I don't suppose they'll listen to other voices in nature. But I have learned a lot from trees: sometimes about the weather, sometimes about animals, sometimes about the Great Spirit.

Walking Buffalo, Stoney

Two Guns

The land ... was put here for us by the Great Spirit and we cannot sell it because it does not belong to us. You can count your money and burn it within the nod of a buffalo's head, but only the Great Spirit can count the grains of sand and the blades of grass of these plains. As a present to you, we will give you anything we have that you can take with you; but the land, never.

A Blackfeet Chief

INDIAN SPIRIT

Remember that your children are not your own, but are lent to you by the Creator.

Mohawk proverb

My sun is set. My day is done. Darkness is stealing over me. Before I lie down to rise no more, I will speak to my people, Hear me, my friends, for it is not the time for me to tell you a lie. The Great Spirit made us, the Indians, and gave us this land we live in. He gave us the buffalo, the antelope, and the deer for food and clothing....

We fought our enemies and feasted our friends. Our braves drove away all who would take our game.... Our children were many and our herds were large. Our old men talked with spirits and made good medicine. Our young men herded the horses and made love to the girls. Where the tipi was, there we stayed and no house imprisoned us. No one said, "To this line is my land, to that is yours." In this way our fathers lived and were happy.... Then they sang the Indian songs and would be as the Lakotas were and not as the white men are.... Shadows are long and dark before me. I shall soon lie down to rise no more. While my spirit is with my body the smoke of my breath shall be towards the Sun for he knows all things and knows that I am still true to him.

Red Cloud, Oglala Lakota

Red Cloud
Oglala Lakota

INDIAN SPIRIT

The Lakota loved the earth and all things of the earth, the attachment growing with age. The old people came literally to love the soil and they sat or reclined on the ground with a feeling of being close to a mothering power. It was good for the skin to touch the earth and the old people liked to remove their moccasins and walk with bare feet on the sacred earth. Their tipis were built upon the earth and their altars were made of earth.... It was the final abiding place of all things that lived and grew. The soil was soothing, strengthening, cleansing, and healing.

That is why the old Indian still sits upon the earth instead of propping himself up and away from its life-giving forces. For him, to sit or lie upon the ground is to be able to think more deeply and to feel more keenly; he can see more clearly into the mysteries of life and come closer in kinship to other lives about him....

The old Lakota was wise. He knew that man's heart away from nature becomes hard; he knew that lack of respect for growing, living things soon led to lack of respect for humans too. So he kept his youth close to its softening influence.

Standing Bear
Oglala Lakota

Old Person
Piegan Blackfeet

Ohiyesa
Wahpeton Dakota

INDIAN SPIRIT

Ohiyesa

The truly brave man, we contend, yields neither to fear nor anger, desire nor agony; he is at all times master of himself.

Ohiyesa
Wahpeton Dakota

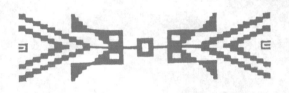

It is commonly supposed that there is no systematic education of their children among the aborigines of this country. Nothing could be farther from the truth. All the customs of this primitive people were held to be divinely instituted, and those in connection with the training of children were scrupulously adhered to and transmitted from one generation to another....

Our manners and morals were not neglected. I was made to respect the adults and especially the aged. I was not allowed to join in their discussions, nor even to speak in their presence, unless requested to do so. Indian etiquette was very strict, and among the requirements was that of avoiding the direct address. A term of relationship or some title of courtesy was commonly used instead of the personal name by those who wished to show respect. We were taught generosity to the poor and reverence for the "Great Mystery." Religion was the basis of all Indian training.

Ohiyesa

INDIAN SPIRIT

My friends, I have been asked to show you my heart. I am glad to have a chance to do so. I want the white people to understand my people. Some of you think an Indian is like the wild animal. This is a great mistake. I will tell you all about our people, and then you can judge whether an Indian is a man or not. I believe much trouble and blood would be saved if we opened our hearts more. I will tell you in my way how the Indian sees things. The white man has more words to tell you how they look to him, but it does not require many words to speak the truth. What I have to say will come from the heart, and I will speak with a straight tongue. The Great Spirit is looking at me, and will hear me....

Our fathers gave us many laws, which they had learned from their fathers. These laws were good. They told us to treat all men as they treated us; that we should never be the first to break a bargain; that it was a disgrace to tell a lie; that we should speak only the truth; that it was a shame for one man to take from another his wife, or his property without paying for it. We were taught to believe that the Great Spirit sees and hears everything, and that He never forgets; that hereafter He will give every man a spirit-home according to his desserts; if he has been a good man, he will have a good home; if he has been a bad man, he will have a bad home. This I believe, and all my people believe the same.

Rolling Thunder (Chief Joseph)
Nez Perce

Sell a country! Why not sell the air, the clouds, and the great sea, as well as the earth? Did not the Great Spirit make them all for the use of His children?

Tecumseh (Shooting Star)
Shawnee

Mosquito Hawk
Assiniboine

Many Horns
Yantonai Nakota

INDIAN SPIRIT

In the long ago the Lakotas were in camp and two young men lay upon a hill watching for signs. They saw a long way in the distance a lone person coming.... When the person came close, they saw that it was a woman and when she came nearer that she was without clothing of any kind except that her hair was very long and fell over her body like a robe. One young man said to the other that he would go and meet the woman and embrace her.... His companion cautioned him to be careful.... But the young man would not be persuaded and met the woman.... His companion saw him attempt to embrace her and there was a cloud closed about them.... In a short time the cloud disappeared and the woman was alone. She beckoned to the other young man and told him to come there and assured him that he would not be harmed....

When he got there, she showed him the bare bones of his companion.... The young man was very much afraid,... but she told him that if he would do as she directed, no harm would come to him.... She then directed him to return to the camp and call all the council together and tell them that in a short time they would see four puffs of smoke under the sun at midday. When they saw this sign they should prepare a feast, and all sit in the customary circle to have the feast served when she would enter the camp, but the men must all sit with their head bowed and look at the ground until she was in their midst. Then she would serve the feast to them and after they had feasted she would tell them what to do: that they must obey her in everything; that if they obeyed her in everything they would have their prayers to the <u>Wakan</u> <u>Tanka</u> answered and be prosperous and happy....

Then she disappeared as a mist disappears so that the young man knew that she was <u>Wakan</u>. He returned to the camp and told these things to the people and the council decided to do as she had instructed the young man.... In a few days they saw four puffs of black smoke under the sun at midday, so they prepared for a feast and all dressed in their best clothing and sat in the circle.... (continued)

(continued)

Every man bowed his head and looked toward the ground. Suddenly the women began uttering low exclamations of admiration…. Then the woman entered the circle and took the food and served it, first to the little children and then to the women and then she bade the men to look up. They did so and saw a very beautiful woman dressed in the softest deerskin which was ornamented with fringes and colors more beautiful than any woman of the Lakota had ever worked…. She told them that she wished to serve them always; that they had first seen her as smoke and that they should always see her as smoke. Then she took from her pouch a pipe and willow bark and Lakota tobacco and filled the pipe with the bark and tobacco and lighted it with a coal of fire.

She smoked a few whiffs and handed the pipe to the chief and told him to smoke and hand it to another. Thus the pipe was passed until all had smoked. She then instructed the council how to gather the bark and the tobacco and prepare it, and gave the pipe into their keeping, telling them that as long as they preserved this pipe she would serve them. But she would serve them in this way. When the smoke came from the pipe she would be present and hear their prayers and take them to the <u>Wakan Tanka</u> and plead for them that their prayers should be answered.

After this she remained in this camp for many days and all the time she was there everyone was happy for she went from tipi to tipi with good words for all. When the time came for her to go, she called all the people together…. She stood in the midst of the circle and when the fire had burned to coals she directed the shaman to place on it the sweetgrass. This made a cloud of smoke and the woman entered the smoke and disappeared…. The shamans instructed the people that they could make other pipes and use them and that (the sacred woman) would be in the smoke of any such pipe if smoked with proper solemnity and form.

Thus it was that the Beautiful Woman brought the pipe to the Lakotas.

Finger, Oglala Lakota

Black Bear
Oglala Lakota

Black Elk
Oglala Lakota

INDIAN SPIRIT

Black Elk

We Indians know the One
true God, and ... we pray
to Him continually.

Black Elk
Oglala Lakota

Mitá, Kola
Heuaka Sápa

Perhaps the most important reason for lamenting* is that it helps us to
realize our oneness with all things, to know that all things are our relatives; and then in behalf of all things we pray to
<u>Wakan</u> <u>Tanka</u> that He may give to us knowledge of
Him who is the source of all things, yet greater than
all things.

Black Elk

* a vision quest

Even to this day the (sacred) pipe is very <u>wakan</u>. Long ago a people were camping and two young men from the camp were going ahead, it is said. They were going along a ridge. Then suddenly a very beautiful woman appeared climbing the hill. She was coming, carrying something. So they stood watching her, it is said. Then one of the young men said, "Well, my friend, I will do it with her." "Look, my friend, see clearly! She is not a woman, probably something <u>wakan</u>," the other said. But the young man was not afraid. So he went there but no further, for from the sky a very big cloud fell on them, it is said. And when it cleared away, the young man was nothing but bones lying there, it is said.

The woman-who-was-not-a-woman was coming in a <u>wakan</u> manner....

So the other young man stood there trembling, it is said. Then the woman said this, "Young man, do not fear me! ... I am bringing home news. I am bringing something so the people will live; it is the Buffalo Calf Pipe. They will live in a <u>wakan</u> manner. I will assist all of the people by showing them good ways." She left saying, "Now after a while, I will arrive bringing news."

So the young man hurried home with the news, it is said. And then the crier took it and since the camp circle was large, the crier walked all around proclaiming the news, it is said. "Howo! Something is coming but it is coming in a <u>wakan</u> manner so no one think anything evil. Follow good ways. In a very <u>wakan</u> manner it comes," the crier proclaimed, it is said. And so all the people prepared themselves, it is said.

Now the woman came among the tipis, it is said. And she told them she had something, it is said. "The Buffalo Calf Pipe arrives here," she said, it is said. "Anyone who does bad deeds and uses this pipe will be rubbed out," she said, it is said. The woman was a very beautiful woman, it is said. She was completely naked, it is said. Her hair was very long, it is said.

Thomas Tyon, Oglala Lakota

White Whirlwind
Oglala Lakota

Afraid of Eagle
Lower Brule Lakota

It is strictly believed and understood by the Sioux that a child is the greatest gift from <u>Wakan Tanka</u>, in response to many devout prayers, sacrifices, and promises. Therefore the child is considered "sent by <u>Wakan Tanka</u>," through some element—namely, the element of human being. That the child may grow up in health with all the virtues expected, and especially that no serious misfortune may befall the child, the father makes promises or vows to <u>Wakan Tanka</u> as manifested by the different elements of the earth and sky. During the period of youthful blessedness the father spared no pains to let the people know of his great love for his child or children. This was measured by his fellow men according to the sacrifices or gifts given, or the number of ceremonies performed. In order to have a standard by which this love could be shown, the first thing taken into consideration and adopted was the White Buffalo Maiden, sent to the Sioux tribe by the Buffalo tribe. The impression left upon the people by the Maiden and her extraordinary good qualities were things that were much admired by every parent as a model for his children. This Maiden was pure white, without a blemish—that was the principal desire of the father for the character of his child. The Maiden addressed men, women, and children.

... It had been told by the Maiden that good things would come to the people by means of the pipe, so it seemed necessary that there be a ceremony, having connection with the Maiden and with the pipe. For this reason the essential article in the "investiture" ceremony is the "ceremonial pipe," a decorated wand, which represents the pipe given to the Indians by the Maiden, the original pipe not being available when needed for this ceremony. (continued)

INDIAN SPIRIT

(continued)

    This wand, or pipestem, was carried and employed by the leader during the ceremony, and when that was finished it was given to the child for whom the ceremony had been performed. In many families such a pipestem was handed down for many generations. The manner of decorating the pipestem has also been handed down, and neither the shape nor the decoration can be changed. A new pipestem might be made by some one who had undergone the ceremony, but an old one was generally used.... The tail feathers of an eagle, in the form of a fan, and also strands of horsehair, were hung from the wand.

High Eagle, Hunkpapa Lakota

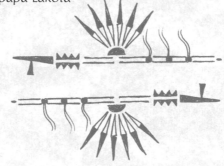

    I have spoken before about the sacred support that was always present for the traditional Indians. With this support everywhere, from the moment you arose and said your first prayer, until the moment you went to sleep, you could at least see what was necessary in order to lead a proper life. Even the dress that you wore every day had sacred meanings, such as the bead work designs on the clothing, and wherever you went or whatever you did, whether you were hunting, making weapons, or whatever you were doing, you were participating in a sacred life and you knew who you were and carried a sense of the sacred with you. All of the forms had meaning, even the tipi and the sacred circle of the entire camp. Of course the life was hard and difficult and not all Indians followed the rules. But the support of the traditional life and the presence of Nature everywhere brought great blessings on all the people.

Yellowtail, Absaroke

Three Fingers
Southern Cheyenne

Jack Red Cloud
Oglala Lakota

INDIAN SPIRIT

It was our belief that the love of possessions is a weakness to be overcome. Its appeal is to the material part, and if allowed its way it will in time disturb the spiritual balance of the man.

Ohiyesa
Wahpeton Dakota

James Red Cloud
Oglala Lakota

The attitude of the Indian toward death, the test and background of life, is entirely consistent with his character and philosophy. Death has no terror for him; he meets it with simplicity and perfect calm, seeking only an honorable end as his last gift to his family and descendants.

Ohiyesa

Jack Red Cloud

Naturally magnanimous and open-minded, the red man prefers to believe that the Spirit of God is not breathed into man alone, but that the whole created universe is a sharer in the immortal perfection of its Maker.

Ohiyesa

INDIAN SPIRIT

I am going to light the pipe and talk to the Great Spirit. (He lighted the pipe, and, looking up reverently, said:) The Great Spirit has made the red man and the white man, and sees all before Him today. Have pity upon us! May the white man and the Indian speak truth to each other today. The sun that looks down upon us today, and gives us light and heat, sees that our hearts are true, and that what we do is good for the poor red man. The moon, that shines on us in the night-time, will see us prosper and do well. The earth, on which we walk, from which we come, and which we love as our mother—which we love as our country—we ask Thee to see that we do that which is good for us and our children. This tobacco comes from the whites; we mix it with bark from the Indian trees and burn it together before Thee, O Great Spirit! So may our hearts and the hearts of the white men go out together to Thee and be made good and right.

Black Foot (Sits in the Middle of the Land), Absaroke

Black Foot
Absaroke

Heebe-Tee-Tse
Shoshone

Wakan Tanka, pity me. In the name of the nation, I offer You this pipe. Wherever the Sun, Moon, Earth, and Four Winds are, there You are always. Father, save these people, I beg You. We wish to live! Guard us against all misfortunes and calamities. Take pity.

Sitting Bull
Hunkpapa Lakota

I am bothered what to believe. Some years ago a good man, as I think, came to us. He talked me out of all my old faith; and after a while, thinking that he must know more of these matters than an ignorant Indian, I joined his church, and became a Methodist. After a while he went away; another man came and talked, and I became a Baptist; then another came and talked, and I became a Presbyterian. Now another one has come, and wants me to be an Episcopalian. All these people tell different stories, and each wants me to believe that his special way is the only way to be good and save my soul. I have about made up my mind that either they all lie, or that they don't know any more about it than I did at first. I have always believed in the Great Spirit, and worshiped him in my own way. These people don't seem to want to change my belief in the Great Spirit, but to change my way of talking to him. White men have education and books, and ought to know exactly what to do, but hardly any two of them agree on what should be done.

Spotted Tail, Brule Lakota

INDIAN SPIRIT

We are thankful that so many of us are alive to meet together here once more, and that we are ready to hold our ceremonies in good faith. Now we shall meet here twelve nights in succession to pray to Our Creator, who has directed us to worship in this way. And these twelve spirits (<u>mesingw</u>) are here to watch and to carry our prayers to Our Creator in the highest heaven. The reason why we dance at this time is to raise our prayers to Him.

When we come into this house of ours we are glad, and thankful that we are well, and for everything that makes us feel good that the Creator has placed here for our use. We come here to pray Him to have mercy on us for the year to come and to give us everything to make us happy. We all realize what He has put before us all through life, and that He has given us a way to pray to Him and thank Him.

We are thankful to the East because everyone feels good in the morning when they awake, and sees the bright light coming from the East, and when the Sun goes down in the West we feel good and glad we are well; then we are thankful to the West. And we are thankful to the North, because when the cold winds come we are glad to have lived to see the leaves fall again; and to the South, for when the south wind blows and everything is coming up in the spring, we are glad to live to see the grass growing and everything green again. We thank the Thunders, for they are the spirits (<u>manitous</u>) that bring the rain, which the Creator has given them power to rule over. And we thank our mother, the Earth, whom we claim as mother because the Earth carries us and everything we need. When we eat and drink and look around, we know it is Our Creator that makes us feel good that way. He gives us the purest thoughts that can be had. We should pray to Him every morning.

Man has a spirit, and the body seems to be a coat for that spirit. That is why people should take care of their spirits, so as to reach Heaven and be admitted to the Creator's dwelling. We are given some length of time to live on earth, and then our spirits must go. When anyone's time comes to leave this earth, he should go to the Creator, feeling good on the way. We all ought to pray to Him, to prepare ourselves for days to come so that we can be with Him after leaving the earth.

We must all put our thoughts to this meeting, so that Our Creator will look upon us and grant what we ask. You all come here to pray; you have a way to reach Him all through life. Do not think of evil; strive always to think of the good that He has given us.

꒒꒒꒒

Opening speech of the Delaware Big House Ceremony, Lenape Delaware

34

Kenawash
Chippewa Cree

One Bull
Hunkpapa Lakota

INDIAN SPIRIT

We, the true and traditional religious leaders, recognized as such by the Hopi People, maintain full authority over all land and life contained within the Western Hemisphere. We are granted our stewardship by virtue of our instruction as to the meaning of Nature, Peace, and Harmony as spoken to our People by Him, known to us as <u>Massau'u</u>, the Great Spirit, who long ago provided for us the sacred stone tablets which we preserve to this day. For many generations before the coming of the white man ... the Hopi People have lived in the sacred place known to you as the Southwest and known to us to be the spiritual center of our continent. Those of us of the Hopi Nation who have followed the path of the Great Spirit without compromise have a message which we are committed, through our prophecy, to convey to you.

The white man, through his insensitivity to the way of Nature, has desecrated the face of Mother Earth. The white man's advanced technological capacity has occurred as a result of his lack of regard for the spiritual path and for the way of all living things. The white man's desire for material possessions and power has blinded him to the pain he has caused Mother Earth by his quest for what he calls natural resources. And the path of the Great Spirit has become difficult to see by almost all men, even by many Indians who have chosen instead to follow the path of the white man....

Today the sacred lands where the Hopi live are being desecrated by men who seek coal and water from our soil that they may create more power for the white man's cities. This must not be allowed to continue for if it does, Mother Nature will react in such a way that almost all men will suffer the end of life as they now know it. The Great Spirit said not to allow this to happen even as it was prophesied to our ancestors. The Great Spirit said not to take from the Earth—not to destroy living things. The Great Spirit, <u>Massau'u</u>, said that man was to live in Harmony and maintain a good clean land for all children to come. All Hopi People and other Indian Brothers are standing on this religious principle and the Traditional

(continued)

Slow Bull
Miniconjou Lakota

INDIAN SPIRIT

(continued)

Spiritual Unity Movement today is endeavoring to reawaken the spiritual nature in Indian people throughout this land. Your government has almost destroyed our basic religion which actually is a way of life for all our people in this land of the Great Spirit. We feel that to survive the coming Purification Day, we must return to the basic religious principles and to meet together on this basis as leaders of our people.

Today almost all the prophecies have come to pass. Great roads like rivers pass across the landscape; man talks to man through the cobwebs of telephone lines; man travels along the roads in the sky in his airplanes; two great wars have been waged by those bearing the swastika or the rising sun; man is tampering with the Moon and the stars. Most men have strayed from the path shown us by the Great Spirit. For <u>Massau'u</u> alone is great enough to portray the way back to Him.

It is said by the Great Spirit that if a gourd of ashes is dropped upon the Earth, that many men will die and that the end of this way of life is near at hand. We interpret this as the dropping of atomic bombs on Hiroshima and Nagasaki. We do not want to see this happen to any place or any nation again, but instead we should turn all this energy for peaceful uses, not for war.

We, the religious leaders and rightful spokesmen for the Hopi Independent Nation, have been instructed by the Great Spirit to express the invitation to the President of the United States and all spiritual leaders everywhere to meet with us and discuss the welfare of mankind so that Peace, Unity, and Brotherhood will become part of all men everywhere.

Thomas Banyacya, on behalf of Hopi Traditional Village Leaders

Slow Bull

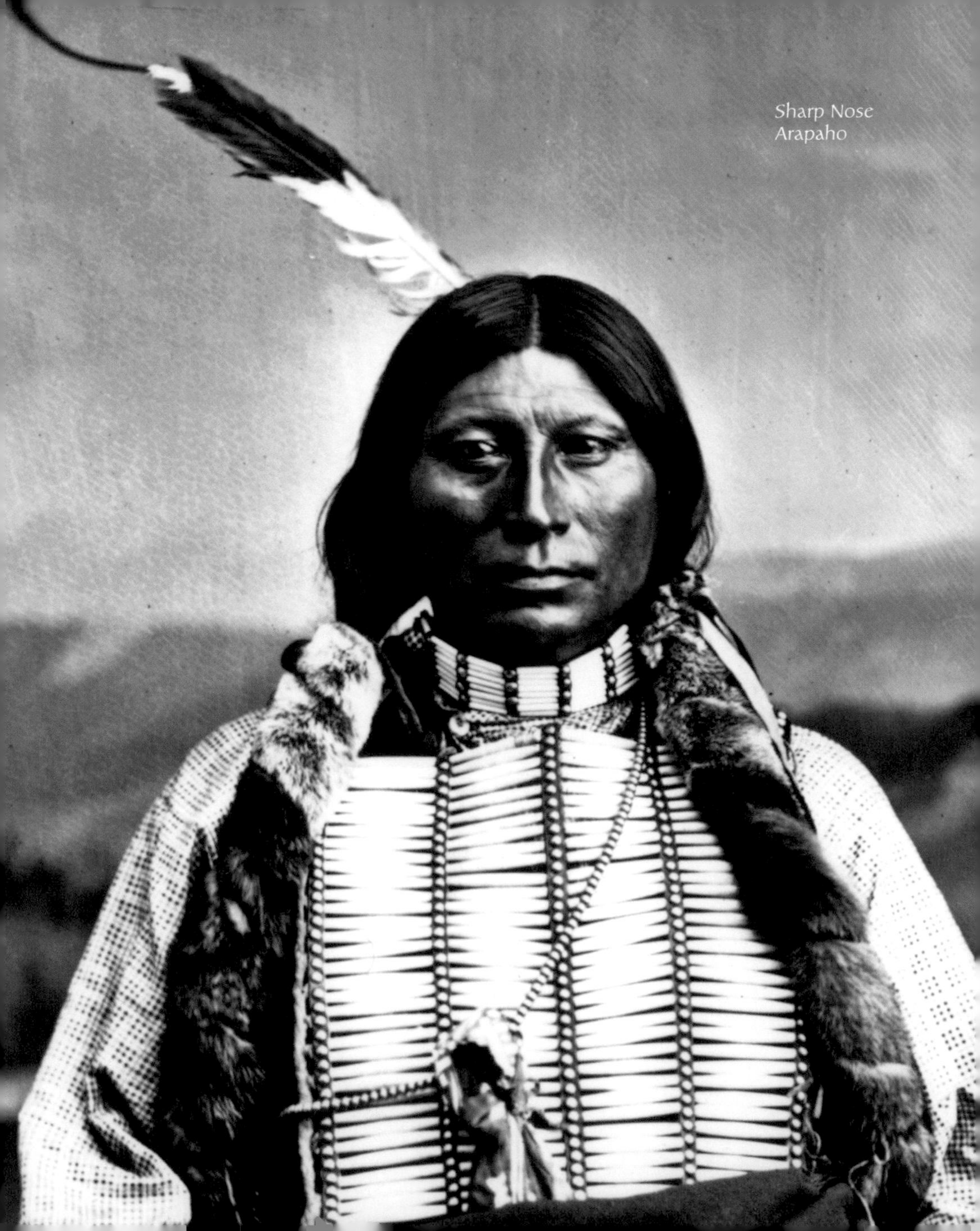
Sharp Nose
Arapaho

INDIAN SPIRIT

Certainly they are a heartless nation. They have made some of their people servants—yes, slaves! We have never believed in keeping slaves, but it seems that these whites do!

The greatest object of their lives seems to be to acquire possessions—to be rich. They desire to possess the whole world. For thirty years they were trying to entice us to sell them our land. Finally the outbreak [Minnesota, 1862] gave them all, and we have been driven away from our beautiful country.

They are a wonderful people. They have divided the day into hours, like the moons of the year. In fact, they measure everything. Not one of them would let so much as a turnip go from his field unless he received full value for it. I understand that their great men make a feast and invite many, but when the feast is over the guests are required to pay for what they have eaten before leaving the house....

I am also informed, but this I hardly believe, that their Great Chief [President] compels every man to pay him for the land he lives upon and all his personal goods—even for his own existence—every year! I am sure we could not live under such a law.

In war they have leaders and war-chiefs of different grades. The common warriors are driven forward like a herd of antelopes to face the foe. It is on account of this manner of fighting—from compulsion and not from personal bravery—that we count no coup on them.

White Footprint, Sioux

Hollow Horn Bear
Brule Lakota

INDIAN SPIRIT

We thank the Great Spirit for all the benefits He has conferred upon us. For myself, I never take a drink of water from a spring, without being mindful of His goodness.

Black Hawk, Sauk

Hollow Horn Bear

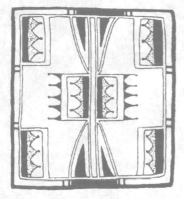

Excessive manners were put down as insincere, and the constant talker was considered rude and thoughtless. Conversation was never begun at once, nor in a hurried manner. No one was quick with a question, no matter how important, and no one was pressed for an answer. A pause giving time for thought was the truly courteous way of beginning and conducting a conversation. Silence was meaningful with the Lakota. Also in the midst of sorrow, sickness, and death, or misfortune of any kind, and in the presence of the notable and great, silence was the mark of respect. More powerful than words was silence with the Lakota.

Standing Bear, Oglala Lakota

Rolling Thunder
(Chief Joseph)
Nez Perce

INDIAN SPIRIT

The Nez Perce began his preparation for spiritual attainment almost in infancy. The child, either boy or girl, when less than ten years of age was told by the father or the mother that it was time to have <u>tiwatit-mas</u>—spiritual power. "This afternoon you must go to yonder mountain and fast. When you reach the place of fasting, build a fire and do not let it die. As the Sun goes down, sit on the rocks facing him, watch while he goes from sight, and look in that direction all night. When the dawn comes, go to the east and watch the Sun return to his people. When he comes to noon, go to the south and sit there, and when he has traveled low again, go to the west where you sat first and watch until he is gone. Then start for your home." After some sacred object, such as a feather, had been tied to the child's clothing, and a few parting words of instruction and encouragement had been given, the little suppliant was sent on its journey.

Rolling Thunder, Nez Perce

Do not wrong or hate your neighbor, for it is not him that you wrong, you wrong yourself.

Thomas Wildcat Alford, Shawnee

Rolling Thunder
(Chief Joseph)

Sword
Oglala Lakota

INDIAN SPIRIT

The pipe was first given to the Lakotas by the God.... The spirit of the God is in the smoke of any pipe if the pipe is smoked in the proper manner.... The filling of the pipe is an important part of the ceremony. One may pray or sing while filling it.... If the pipe is not filled and lighted in this manner, the spirit of the God will not be in the smoke from the pipe. The pipe should be smoked until the contents are all consumed.... The remains in the pipe thus smoked should be emptied into a fire, for if it is emptied on the ground it may be stepped on and this would offend the God.

When a pipe is smoked in this manner, the spirit that is in the smoke goes with it into the mouth and body and then it comes out and goes upward. When this spirit is in the body, it soothes the spirit of the smoker. When it goes upward, it soothes the God. So the God and the spirit are as friends....

The Lakota should smoke the pipe first when considering any matter of importance.... The first rite in any ceremony of the Lakotas should be to smoke the pipe.... When anyone performs a ceremony after he has smoked the pipe, he should please the God so that the God will give attention to the ceremony.

Sword, Oglala Lakota

Thank you, O Great <u>Manitou</u>, that we have lived until now to purify this our House with (cedar) smoke. For that has been the firm rule from ancient times since the beginning, when anyone recalls how fortunate his children are, and when he sees them enjoying good health. And it is the cause of a feeling of happiness when we consider how greatly we are benefited by the benevolence of our Father, the Great <u>Manitou</u>. And also we can feel the strength of our grandfather Fire, which is why we please him when we purify him and take good care of him, and when we feed him this cedar. All of this we offer in prayer to our grandfather, because he has compassion with us when he sees how pitifully we behave while we are pleading with every spirit (<u>manitou</u>) above, where they were created, and with all those all over the earth. Do everything for us, our Father, that we ask of You, Great <u>Manitou</u>, Our Creator.

Prayer before the Fires, Delaware Big House Ceremony

Our religion is the traditions of our ancestors—the dreams of our old men, given them in the solemn hours of night by the Great Spirit; and the visions of our sacred medicine men, and is written in the hearts of our people.

Seattle, Dwamish

The representation of the medicine man as a nude figure is not a mere fancy,... for in many of the religious rites the priest appeared in such manner. This nudity is not without its significance, it typifies the utter helplessness of man, when his strength is contrasted with the power of the Great Spirit. With his best intelligence and greatest skill in the use of his hands, man is powerless to bring into existence even so much as the tiniest flower, while out of the force of the will of the Mysterious One, all things in the heavens and the earth have come into existence with beauty, grandeur, and majesty.

Francis Laflesche, Omaha

Little Soldier
Oglala Lakota

INDIAN SPIRIT

In these six directions is found everything needed for renewal, physical and intellectual growth, and harmony. There is <u>Wakan</u> <u>Tanka</u> himself, God, the "highest and most holy One"; there is <u>Tunkashila</u>, Grandfather, who corresponds to the Son of God; there is Grandmother Earth; and there are the four cardinal directions, moving in order of importance from west to north to east to south. <u>Wakan</u> <u>Tanka</u> is unlimited (infinite), and has given to each of the other directions sacred powers that are their own to impart as they see fit, including such things as purification, joy, good health, growth, endurance, wisdom, inner peace, warmth, and happiness. The directions are holy and mysterious beings. <u>Wakan</u> <u>Tanka</u> remains above them in power, and they are not separated even though they are distinct and identifiable. The powers do the will of God, yet they have a will and intellect of their own. They hear and answer prayers, yet their powers and ways remain mysterious. With them and through them we send our voice to God.

Fools Crow, Oglala Lakota

Sho-We-Tit
Caddo

INDIAN SPIRIT

There is scarcely anything so exasperating to me as the idea that the natives of this country have no sense of humor and no faculty for mirth. This phase of their character is well understood by those whose fortune or misfortune it has been to live among them day in and day out at their homes. I don't believe I ever heard a real hearty laugh away from the Indians' fireside. I have often spent an entire evening in laughing with them until I could laugh no more. There are evenings when the recognized wit or storyteller of the village gives a free entertainment which keeps the rest of the community in a convulsive state until he leaves them. However, Indian humor consists as much in the gestures and inflections of the voice as in words, and is really untranslatable.

Ohiyesa, Wahpeton Dakota

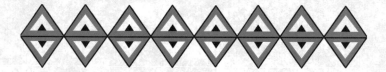

There were no temples or shrines among us save those of nature. Being a natural man, the Indian was intensely poetical. He would deem it sacrilege to build a house for Him who may be met face to face in the mysterious, shadowy aisles of the primeval forest, or on the sunlit bosom of virgin prairies, upon dizzy spires and pinnacles of naked rock, and yonder in the jeweled vault of the night sky! He who enrobes Himself in filmy veils of cloud, there on the rim of the visible world where our Great-Grandfather Sun kindles his evening campfire, He who rides upon the rigorous wind of the north, or breathes forth His spirit upon aromatic southern airs, whose war-canoe is launched upon majestic rivers and inland seas — He needs no lesser cathedral!

Ohiyesa

Many Shots
Piegan Blackfeet

INDIAN SPIRIT

A <u>wakan</u> (holy) man is one who is wise.... It is one who has power with the spirits. It is one who communicates with the spirits.... He knows the ceremonies and the songs. He can tell the people what their visions mean. He can tell the people what the spirits wish them to do. He can tell what is to be in the future. He can talk with animals and with trees and with stones. He can talk with everything on earth.

The <u>Wakan Tanka</u> are those which made everything.... The medicine fathers are all things that are above mankind.... The medicine fathers have power over everything on earth....

Mankind should think about the medicine fathers and do what will please them. They should think of them as they think of their fathers and their mothers....

Animals may be <u>wakan</u>. When an animal is <u>wakan</u>, then mankind should treat it as if it were one of the medicine fathers. Things that do not live may be <u>wakan</u>. When anything is food, it is <u>wakan</u> because it makes life. When anything is medicine, it is <u>wakan</u> for it keeps life in the body....

The songs and the ceremonies of the Oglalas are <u>wakan</u> because they belong to the medicine fathers.... The spirit of every man is <u>wakan</u>.

Little Wound, Oglala Lakota

High Bear
Hunkpapa Lakota

White Man Running Around
Blackfeet

INDIAN SPIRIT

While the prayer with the pipe will start and end the day, it is also important to pray during the day. Each day, whatever I am doing, I am always praying and thinking of God. As I walk along, whether I am out in the field, or wherever, I am always praying.... Acbadadea [the Great Spirit] knows that I pray to Him and He hears me.... I am so used to it that I just can't stop, and I think that it is the best thing a person can do. I say, that if you look for them, then you will find many parts of the day that could be spent in praying. I am sure that there are a lot of people who are that way, continually praying to God, remembering the Name of God.... People think other things are more important than prayer, but they are mistaken. A person may have plenty of money but he doesn't take that along with him [when he dies]. It is good to share what little we have, and pray. A person should measure his wealth in terms of the knowledge and love of God.

Yellowtail, Absaroke

The songs from the Sun Dance were given to our people before history began and these songs link us to our Medicine Fathers and to Acbadadea. As the drum beats, it establishes the heartbeat for the dancers, our tribe, and all of mankind. We feel this link in our hearts and when the drum gives its call and the dancers respond by blowing their eagle bone whistles, we reach into our innermost center, and blessings penetrate all those present at the same time that our prayers rise up to all the universe.

Yellowtail

Wolf Robe
Cheyenne

Wolf Robe

As we smoke the pipe and offer our prayer with each new day, we should remember the importance of having a sacred center within us and that this sacred presence is represented by the pipe. It is the pipe that connects us with Acbadadea. We can no longer have its continual support as the Indians of olden days had; but in our time the pipe may have an even greater importance because some of our other supports are gone, and it remains with us as one of our key blessings.

Yellowtail, Absaroke

Just as the traditional Indians could not depend on someone else to do their work, they did not depend on someone else to say their prayers. Every day, in whatever they did, they lived in a sacred manner. Each of these things may seem small, but it is a series of small things that make up our lives.

Yellowtail

INDIAN SPIRIT

Every part of this soil is sacred in the estimation of my people. Every hillside, every valley, every plain and grove, has been hallowed by some sad or happy event in days long vanished. The very dust upon which you now stand responds more lovingly to their footsteps than to yours, because it is rich with the blood of our ancestors and our bare feet are conscious of the sympathetic touch. Even the little children who lived here and rejoiced here for a brief season will love these somber solitudes and at eventide they greet shadowy returning spirits. And when the last Red Man shall have perished, and the memory of my tribe shall have become a myth among the White Men, these shores will swarm with the invisible dead of my tribe, and when your children's children think themselves alone in the field, the store, the shop, upon the highway, or in the silence of the pathless woods, they will not be alone. At night when the streets of your cities and villages are silent and you think them deserted, they will throng with the return-ing hosts that once filled and still love this beautiful land. The White Man will never be alone.

Let him be just and deal kindly with my people, for the dead are not power-less. Dead, did I say? There is no death, only a change of worlds.

Seattle, Dwamish

Curley Bear
Blackfeet

Dull Knife
Cheyenne

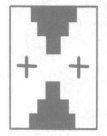

We should understand well that all things are the work of the Great Spirit. We should know that He is within all things: the trees, the grasses, the rivers, the mountains, and all the four-legged animals, and the winged peoples; and even more important, we should understand that He is also above all these things and peoples. When we do understand all this deeply in our hearts, then we will fear, and love, and know the Great Spirit, and then we will be and act and live as He intends.

Black Elk, Oglala Lakota

Since the drum is often the only instrument used in our sacred rites, I should perhaps tell you here why it is especially sacred and important to us. It is because the round form of the drum represents the whole universe, and its steady strong beat is the pulse, the heart, throbbing at the center of the universe. It is as the voice of Wakan Tanka, and this sound stirs us and helps us to understand the mystery and power of all things.

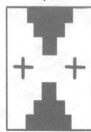

Black Elk

Unknown
Oglala Lakota

Friend and brother! It was the will of the Great Spirit that we should meet together this day. He orders all things, and has given us a fine day for our council. He has taken his garment from before the sun and caused it to shine with brightness upon us. For all these things we thank the Great ruler, and Him ONLY!

Brother, this council-fire was kindled by you. It was at your request that we came together at this time. We have listened with joy to what you have said. You requested us to speak our minds freely....

Brother, listen to what we say. There was a time when our forefathers owned this great island. Their seat extended from the rising to the setting sun. The Great Spirit had made it for the use of the Indians. He had created the buffalo, the deer and other animals for food. He had made the bear and beaver. Their skins served us for clothing. He had scattered them over the country and taught us how to take them. He had caused the earth to produce corn for bread. All this He had done for His red children because He loved them.

Brothers, our seats were once large, and yours were small. You have now become a great people, and we have scarcely a place left to spread our blankets. You have got our country, but are not satisfied; you want to force your religion upon us.

Brother, continue to listen. You say that you are sent to instruct us how to worship the Great Spirit agreeable to His mind; and if we do not take hold of the religion which you white people teach, we shall be unhappy hereafter. You say that you are right, and we are lost. How do we know this to be true? We understand that your religion is written in a book. If it was intended for us as well as you, why has not the Great Spirit given to us—and not only to us, but to our forefathers—the knowledge of that book, with the means of understanding it rightly? We only know what you tell us about it. How shall we know when to believe, being so often deceived by the white people? (continued)

(continued)

Brother, you say there is but one way to worship and serve the Great Spirit. If there is but one religion, why do you white people differ so much about it? Why not all agree, as you can all read the book?

Brother, we do not understand these things. We are told that your religion was given to your forefathers, and has been handed down from father to son. We also have a religion which was given to our forefathers, and has been handed down to us, their children. We worship in that way. It teaches us to be thankful for all favors we receive; to love each other, and be united. We never quarrel about religion, because it is a matter which concerns each man and the Great Spirit.

Brother, we do not wish to destroy your religion or take it from you; we only want to enjoy our own.

Brother, we have been told that you have been preaching to the white people in this place. These people are our neighbors: We are acquainted with them. We will wait a little while and see what effect your preaching has upon them. If we find it does them good, makes them honest and less disposed to cheat Indians, we will consider again of what you have said.

Brother, you have now heard our talk and this is all we have to say at present. As we are going to part, we will come and take you by the hand, and hope the Great Spirit will protect you on your journeys and return you safely to your friends.

Red Jacket, Seneca

Iron Scare
Blackfeet Lakota

Black Bird
Oglala Lakota

INDIAN SPIRIT

Black Bird

The warriors went on the warpath for the protection of the tribe and its hunting grounds. All the people shared in this benefit, so when the warrior fulfilled his vow he wanted all the tribe to share in its benefits. He believed that <u>Wakan Tanka</u> is more ready to grant the requests of those who make vows and fulfill them than of those who are careless of all their obligations; also that an act performed publicly is more effective than the same thing done privately. So when a man was fulfilling his vow, he prayed for all the members of the tribe and for all the branches of the tribe, wherever they might be.

Red Bird, Lakota

INDIAN SPIRIT

All of the best clothing was taken along with him when any warrior set out upon a search for conflict. If a battle seemed about to occur, the warrior's first important preparatory act was to jerk off all his ordinary clothing. He then hurriedly got out his fine garments. If he had time to do so he rebraided his hair, painted his face in his own particular way, did everything needful to prepare himself for presenting the most splendid personal appearance. That is, he got himself ready to die.

The idea of full dress in preparation for a battle comes not from a belief that it will add to the fighting ability. The preparation is for death, in case that should be the result of the conflict. Every Indian wants to look his best when he goes to meet the Great Spirit....

The naked fighters, among the Cheyennes and Sioux, were such warriors as specially fortified themselves by prayer and other devotional exercises. They had special instruction from medicine men. Their naked bodies were painted in peculiar ways, each according to the direction of his favorite spiritual guide, and each had his own medicine charm given to him by this guide. A warrior thus made ready for battle was supposed to be proof against the weapons of the enemy. He placed himself in the forefront of the attack or the defense. His thought was: "I am so protected by my medicine that I do not need to dress for death. No bullet nor arrow can harm me now."

Wooden Leg
Northern Cheyenne

Little Hawk
Oglala Lakota

American Horse
Oglala Lakota

INDIAN SPIRIT

American Horse

The Sun Dance is the greatest ceremony that the Oglalas do. It is a sacred ceremony in which all the people have a part.... It must be conducted by a shaman who knows all the customs of the people. He must know all the secret things of the shamans....

The Sun Dance must be done in a dance lodge made for that purpose. This lodge must not be used for any other purpose.

... The Sun Dance must be done around a sacred pole. This pole must be at the center of the dance lodge.... One who wishes to dance the Sun Dance should make this known some time before the time for doing the dance.... One who wishes to dance the Sun Dance must give feasts and many presents. He must give away all that he possesses. His people must give feasts and presents. He must choose someone to instruct him for the dance. The one he chooses becomes his grandfather. He must think and act just as his grandfather tells him. He must submit to his grandfather in everything until he dances. He must obey the rules for one who is about to dance this dance....

The ceremony of the Sun Dance is in four parts. One part for the dancer and the people to prepare for the dance; one part to gather at the place for the dance; one part for the camp and the ceremonies before the dance; the last part for the Sun Dance.

American Horse, Little Wound, and Lone Star
Oglala Lakota

The ground on which we stand is sacred ground. It is the dust and blood of our ancestors.

Plenty Coups, Absaroke

Their (white man's) wise ones said we might have their religion, but when we tried to understand it we found that there were too many kinds of religion among white men for us to understand, and that scarcely any two white men agreed which was the right one to learn. This bothered us a good deal until we saw that the white man did not take his religion any more seriously than he did his laws, and that he kept both of them just behind him, like helpers, to use when they might do him good in his dealings with strangers. These were not our ways. We kept the laws we made and lived our religion. We have never been able to understand the white man, who fools nobody but himself.

Plenty Coups

Plenty Coups
Absaroke

Yellow Kidney
Piegan

INDIAN SPIRIT

Mother Nature is all-powerful, and eternity is on her side. What are the inventions of man, the lofty cities which he raises on the borders of the desert, the terrible weapons that he uses to realize and defend his conquests? Nothing, but a little heaped-up dust which the great natural forces always tend to restore to its primeval form. Forsake the citadel for a few years, abandon the canon or machine gun for a few months in the prairie, and soon grass and brambles will have overgrown the stones, and rust corroded the hard steel. In how many former times have vast solitudes been peopled by powerful cities! Of them today remain no more than the ruins, and the ruins themselves finally disappear back into the eternally virgin earth. Of what importance are the men who pass? The Spirit has only to blow on them and they will be no more! Then the sons of the Earth will repossess the Earth. And the past time will begin over again as the new time!

Ghost Dancers at Wounded Knee
South Dakota (place of the infamous Sioux massacre in 1890)

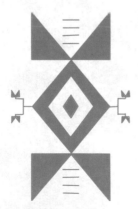

At least one of the lodges in the village makes a feast daily for the Great Spirit. I cannot explain this so that the white people will comprehend me, because we have no regular standard among us. Everyone makes his feast as he thinks best, to please the Great Spirit, who has the care of all beings created.

Black Hawk, Sauk

INDIAN SPIRIT

The last council we had with them, we promised that, in case any more of their people were killed by ours, instead of presents, we would give up the person, or persons, that had done the injury. We made this determination known to our people; but, notwithstanding, one of our young men killed an Ioway the following winter....

We all bid farewell to our young brave, who entered the village alone, singing his death-song, and sat down in the square in the middle of the village. One of the Ioway chiefs came out to us. We told him that we had fulfilled our promise—that we had brought the brother of the young man who had killed one of their people—that he had volunteered to come in his place, in consequence of his brother being unable to travel from sickness. We had no further conversation, but mounted our horses and rode off.... We took our trail back, and traveled until dark.... We had not been here long, before we heard the sound of horses coming towards us.... It was our young brave with two horses. He told me that after we had left him, they menaced him with death for some time—then gave him something to eat— smoked the pipe with him—and made him a present of the two horses and some goods, and started him after us. When we arrived at our village, our people were much pleased; and for the noble and generous conduct of the Ioways, on this occasion, not one of their people has been killed since by any of our nation.

Black Hawk, Sauk

Broken Arm

78

Broken Arm
Oglala Lakota

Black Man
Arapaho

INDIAN SPIRIT

The Great Spirit spoke to us saying:

Take this message to my red children and tell it to them as I say it. I have neglected the Indians for many moons, but I will make them my people now if they obey me in this message. The earth is getting old, and I will make it new for my chosen people, the Indians, who are to inhabit it, and among them will be all those of their ancestors who have died, their fathers, mothers, brothers, cousins, and wives—all those who hear my voice and my words through the tongues of my children.

I will cover the earth with new soil to a depth of five times the height of a man, and under this new soil will be buried all the whites, and all the holes and the rotten places will be filled up. The new lands will be covered with sweet-grass and running water and trees, and herds of buffalo and ponies will stray over it, that my red children may eat and drink, hunt and rejoice.... And while I am making the new earth the Indians who have heard this message and who dance and pray and believe will be taken up in the air and suspended there, while the wave of new earth is passing; then set down among the ghosts of their ancestors, relatives, and friends. Those of my children who doubt will be left in undesirable places, where they will be lost and wander around until they believe and learn the songs and the dance of the ghosts....

Go then, my children, and tell these things to all the people and make all ready for the coming of the ghosts....

Kicking Bear, Miniconjou Lakota
(from one of the visions responsible for the Ghost Dance)

INDIAN SPIRIT

The Sioux are raised with the Sun Dance, and it is the highest expression of our religion. All share in the fasting, in the prayer, and in the benefits. Some in the audience pray along silently with the dancers.... Everyone is profoundly involved, and because of this the Sioux nation and all of the peoples of the world are blessed by Wakan Tanka.

Fools Crow, Oglala Lakota

We did not ask you white men to come here. The Great Spirit gave us this country as a home.... The Great Spirit gave us plenty of land to live on, and buffalo, deer, antelope, and other game.... The Great Spirit did not make us to work, but to live by hunting. You white men can work if you want to. We do not interfere with you, and again you say, why do you not become civilized? We do not want your civilization! We would live as our fathers did, and their fathers before them.

Crazy Horse
Oglala Lakota

Those who are healed do not talk about it among themselves and spread the news. That is not the Sioux way. If a thing is holy and sacred, if it is a miracle, it is not talked about. It is too special for that. Visions we receive are in the same category. They are something personal between Wakan Tanka and the seeker that affects the whole of his life. Even the person's family will not discuss it or tell their friends.

Fools Crow

White Man
Kiowa-Apache

Two Moons
Northern Cheyenne

INDIAN SPIRIT

What is life? It is a flash of a firefly in the night. It is a breath of a buffalo in the winter time. It is as the little shadow that runs across the grass and loses itself in the sunset.

Crowfoot, Blackfeet

As a child I was taught the Supernatural Powers were powerful and could do strange things; that I should placate them and win their favor; that they could help me or harm me; that they could be good friends or harmful enemies. I was taught that the Sun was a Great Mystery, that <u>Wakan</u> <u>Tanka</u> was the Supreme Mystery.... This was taught to me by the wise men and the shamans. They taught me that I could gain their favor by being kind to my people and brave before my enemies; by telling the truth and living straight; by fighting for my people and their hunting grounds.

When the Lakotas believed these things they lived happy and they died satisfied. What more than this can that which the white man offers us give?

The Great Mystery is familiar with my spirit and when I die I will go with him. Then I will be with my forefathers. If this is not in the heaven of the white man, I shall be satisfied. The Sun is my father. The <u>Wakan</u> <u>Tanka</u> of the white man has overcome him. But I shall remain true to him.

Red Cloud, Oglala Lakota

Cuts the Bear's Ears
Absaroke

INDIAN SPIRIT

The Indian conceived an eager desire to learn wisdom from the Master of Life; but, being ignorant where to find him, he had recourse to fasting, dreaming, and magical incantations. By these means it was revealed to him, that, by moving forward in a straight, undeviating course, he would reach the abode of the Great Spirit.... The Great Spirit bade him be seated, and thus addressed him: "I am the Maker of heaven and earth, the trees, lakes, rivers, and all things else. I am the Maker of mankind; and because I love you, you must do My will. The land on which you live I have made for you, and not for others. Why do you suffer the white men to dwell among you? My children, you have forgotten the customs and traditions of your forefathers. Why do you not clothe yourselves in skins, as they did, and use the bows and arrows, and the stone-pointed lances, which they used? You have bought guns, knives, kettles, and blankets from the white men, until you can no longer do without them; and, what is worse, you have drunk the poison fire-water, which turns you into fools. Fling all these things away; live as your wise forefathers lived before you."

Pontiac, Ottawa

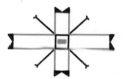

Whenever, in the course of the daily hunt, the red hunter comes upon a scene that is strikingly beautiful and sublime—a black thunder-cloud with the rainbow's glowing arch above the mountain; a white waterfall in the heart of a green gorge; a vast prairie tinged with the blood-red of sunset—he pauses for an instant in the attitude of worship. He sees no need for setting apart one day in seven as a holy day, since to him all days are God's.

Ohiyesa, Wahpeton Dakota

Little Bird

The Sun Dance is so sacred to us that we do not talk of it often.... The cutting of the bodies in fulfillment of a Sun Dance vow is different from the cutting of the flesh when people are in sorrow. A man's body is his own, and when he gives his body or his flesh he is giving the only thing which really belongs to him.

Chased by Bears
Yanktonai Dakota

When a man does a piece of work which is admired by all we say that it is wonderful; but when we see the changes of day and night, the sun, the moon, and the stars in the sky, and the changing seasons upon the earth, with their ripening fruits, anyone must realize that it is the work of someone more powerful than man.

Chased by Bears

Little Bird
Southern Arapaho

INDIAN SPIRIT

I shall vanish and be no more,
But the land over which I now roam
Shall remain
And change not.

Song of the Hethushka Warrior
Society, Omaha

There is a great deal in what a man believes, and if a man's religion is changed for the better or for the worse he will know it. The Sun Dance was our first and our only religion. We believed that there is a mysterious power greater than all others, which is represented by nature, one form of representation being the sun. Thus we made sacrifices to the sun, and our petitions were granted. The Indians lived longer in the old days than now. I would not say this change is due to throwing away the old religion; there may be other reasons, but in the old times the Sun Dance was held annually and was looked forward to with eagerness. I believe we had true faith at that time.

Red Bird, Lakota

Long Feather
Hunkpapa Lakota

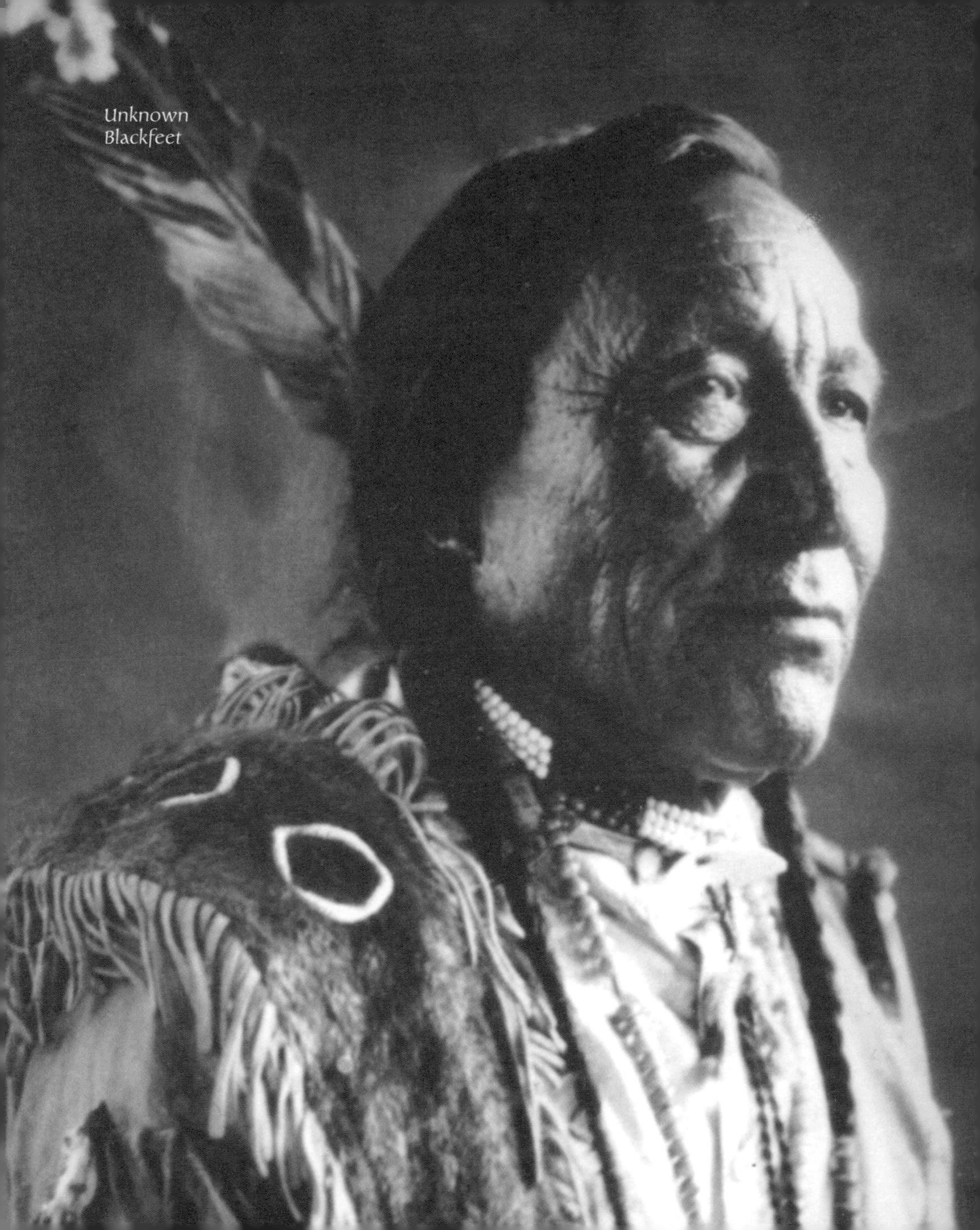

Unknown
Blackfeet

INDIAN SPIRIT

Well, now I shall tell you about this which we sing. As we sing the <u>Manitou</u> hears us. The <u>Manitou</u> will not fail to hear us. It is just as if we were singing within the <u>Manitou's</u> dwellings … We are not singing sportive songs. It is as if we are weeping, asking for life.

Owl, Fox

We now do crown you with the sacred emblem of the deer's antlers, the emblem of your Lordship. You shall now become a mentor of the people of the Five Nations. The thickness of your skin shall be seven span—which is to say that you shall be proof against anger, offensive actions, and criticism. Your heart shall be filled with peace and good will and your mind filled with a yearning for the welfare of the people of the Confederacy. With endless patience you shall carry out your duty and your firmness shall be tempered with tenderness for your people. Neither anger nor fury shall find lodgement in your mind and all your words and actions shall be marked with calm deliberation. In all of your deliberations in the Confederate Council, in your efforts at law-making, in all your official acts, self-interest shall be cast into oblivion. Cast not over your shoulder behind you the warnings of the nephews and nieces should they chide you for any error or wrong you may do, but return to the way of the Great Law which is just and right. Look and listen for the welfare of the whole people and have always in view not only the present but also the coming generations, even those whose faces are yet beneath the surface of the ground —the unborn of the future Nation.

Instructions to new members of the Five Nation Confederate Lords, Iroquois Constitution

INDIAN SPIRIT

When a man cries for a vision, it is nearly like the Sun Dance.... He takes a pipe filled with tobacco to the lodge of a holy man.... Then the holy man takes the pipe and smokes it, it is said.... And then the holy man says.... "When a man cries for a vision, from that time on he can think nothing bad. Try to live well! My friend, later, in this way, I will prepare you," he says....

Now he builds a sweat lodge. Now the man who will cry for a vision goes there, it is said.... Inside the sweat lodge everything is well covered with a blanket of sage, it is said. Now the vision quester goes into the lodge, it is said.... And they cover the door; then they pray very earnestly, it is said.... So the holy man instructs the vision quester.... "Stand with a strong heart! In this way you will become <u>wakan</u>." Saying this, he instructs him, it is said. "Pray to inquire wisely and well into everything!"...

So now the vision quester, wearing only a furred robe around his shoulders and with a pipe and kinnikinic, carrying a filled pipe and wearing the robe, he stands ready, they say. The bowl of the pipe that he carries is sealed with tallow, it is said. Thus the tobacco will not be scattered. So it is....

Now the vision quester wraps the robe around himself with the fur side out, and until the sun rises, he stands looking east, pointing with the pipe that he holds, praying as hard as he can. All night long he stands in this way, it is said. At last the dawn seems to be visible and so he stands, rejoicing greatly, it is said.

Thomas Tyon, Oglala Lakota

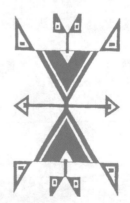

The grandfathers and
the grandmothers
are in the children:
teach them well.

Ojibwa proverb

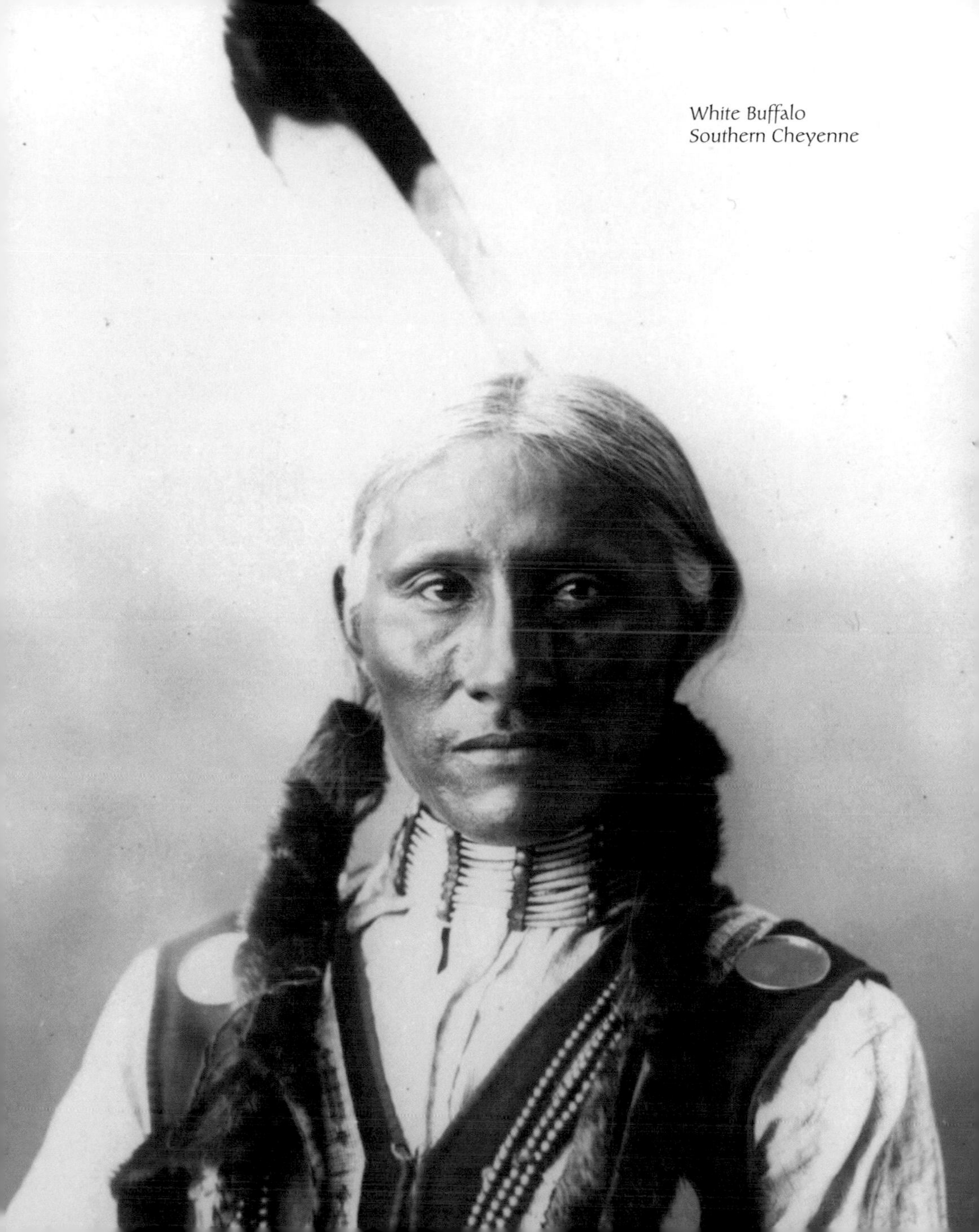

White Buffalo
Southern Cheyenne

Yellow Shirt
Brule Lakota

Regarding the "civilization" that has been thrust upon me since the days of the reservation, it has not added one whit to my sense of justice; to my reverence for the rights of life; to my love for truth, honesty, and generosity; nor to my faith in <u>Wakan Tanka</u>—God of the Lakotas. For after all the great religions have been preached and expounded, or have been revealed by brilliant scholars, or have been written in books and embellished in fine language with finer covers, man—all man—is still confronted with the Great Mystery.

So if today I had a young mind to direct, to start on the journey of life, and I was faced with the duty of choosing between the natural way of my forefathers and that of the white man's present way of civilization, I would, for its welfare, unhesitatingly set that child's feet in the path of my forefathers. I would raise him to be an Indian!

Standing Bear, Oglala Lakota

Yellow Shirt

INDIAN SPIRIT

I wonder if the ground has anything to say? I wonder if the ground is listening to what is said? I wonder if the ground would come alive and what is on it? Though I hear what the ground says. The ground says, "It is the Great Spirit that placed me here." The Great Spirit tells me to take care of the Indians, to feed them aright. The Great Spirit appointed the roots to feed the Indians on. The water says the same thing. The Great Spirit directs me, "Feed the Indians well." The grass says the same thing, "Feed the Indians well." The ground, water, and grass say, "The Great Spirit has given us our names. We have these names and hold these names." The ground says, "The Great Spirit has placed me here to produce all that grows on me, trees and fruit." The same way the ground says, "It was from me man was made." The Great Spirit, in placing men on the earth, desired them to take good care of the ground and to do each other no harm.

Young Chief, Cayuse

The first American mingled with his pride a singular humility. Spiritual arrogance was foreign to his nature and teaching. He never claimed that the power of articulate speech was proof of superiority over the dumb creation; on the other hand, it is to him a perilous gift. He believes profoundly in silence—the sign of a perfect equilibrium. Silence is the absolute poise or balance of body, mind, and spirit. The man who preserves his selfhood is ever calm and unshaken by the storms of existence—not a leaf, as it were, astir on the tree; not a ripple upon the surface of the shining pool—his, in the mind of the unlettered sage, is the ideal attitude and conduct of life.

If you ask him: "What is silence?" he will answer: "It is the Great Mystery!" "The holy silence is His voice!" If you ask: "What are the fruits of silence?" he will say: "They are self-control, true courage or endurance, patience, dignity, and reverence." Silence is the cornerstone of character.

Ohiyesa
Wahpeton Dakota

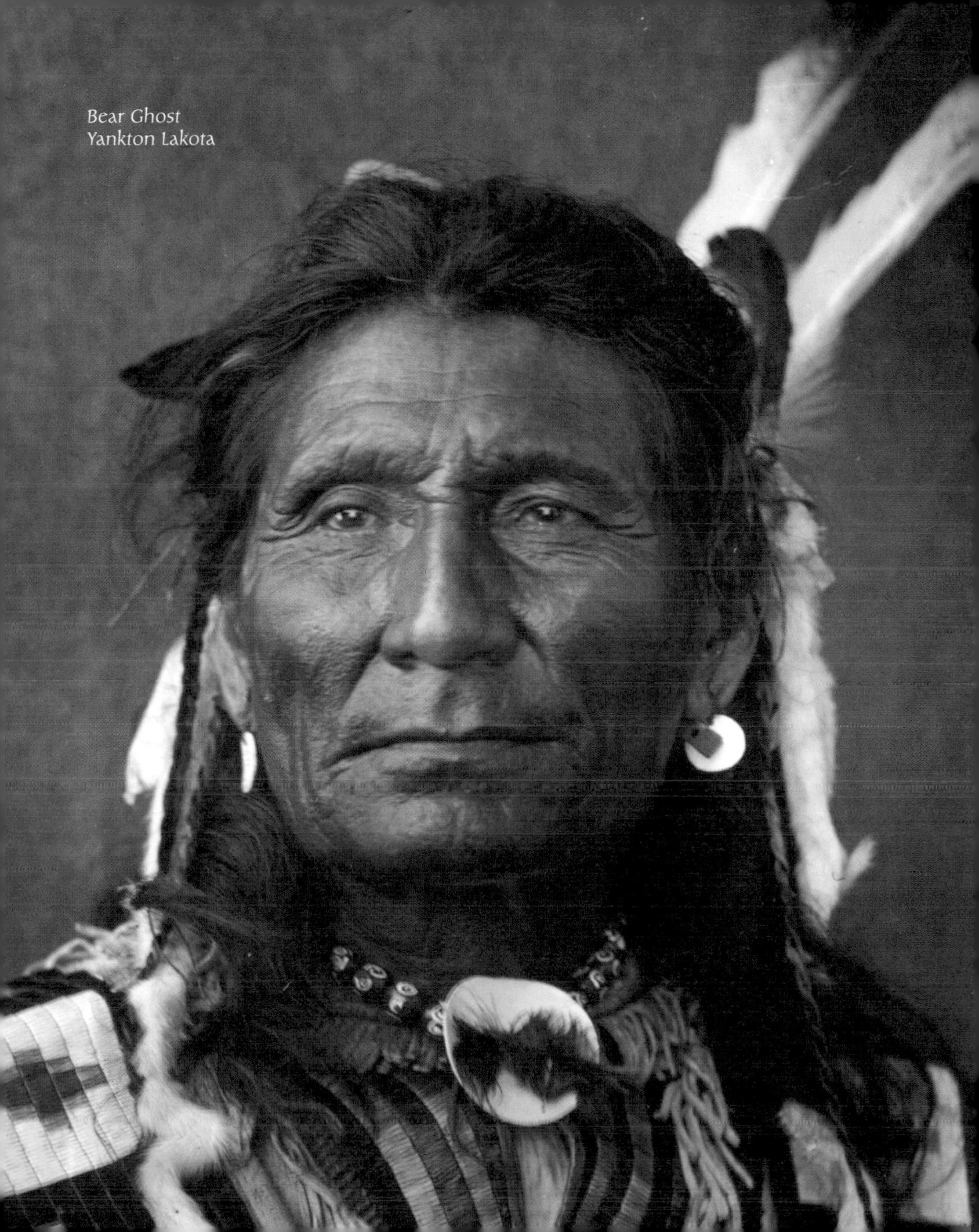

Bear Ghost
Yankton Lakota

Sitting Bull
Hunkpapa Lakota

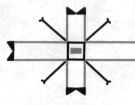

Behold, my brothers, the spring has come; the earth has received the embraces of the sun and we shall soon see the results of that love!

Every seed is awakened and so has all animal life. It is through this mysterious power that we too have our being and we therefore yield to our neighbors, even our animal neighbors, the same right as ourselves, to inhabit this land.

Sitting Bull, Hunkpapa Lakota

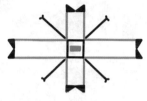

Sitting Bull

All the Indians pray to God for life, and try to find out a good road, and do nothing wrong in this life. This is what we want, and to pray to God. But you did not believe us.

You should say nothing against our religion, for we say nothing against yours. You pray to God. So do all of us Indians, as well as the Whites. We both pray to only one God, who made us all.

Sitting Bull

INDIAN SPIRIT

For the Great Spirit is everywhere; He hears whatever is in our minds and hearts, and it is not necessary to speak to Him in a loud voice.

Black Elk
Oglala Lakota

With this sacred pipe you will walk upon the Earth; for the Earth is your Grandmother and Mother, and She is sacred. Every step that is taken upon Her should be as a prayer. The bowl of this pipe is of red stone; it is the Earth.... The stem of the pipe is of wood, and this represents all that grows upon Earth.... All the things of the universe are joined to you who smoke the pipe—all send their voices to <u>Wakan</u> <u>Tanka</u>, the Great Spirit. When you pray with this pipe, you pray for and with everything.

Black Elk

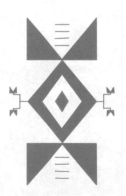

Hey-a-a-hey! Hey-a-a-hey! Hey-a-a-hey! Grandfather, the Great Spirit, behold me on earth. It is said that You lived first. You are older than all the prayers that are sent to You. All things on earth, the four-leggeds, the wings of the air, belong to You. It is said that You have made all things. Also, You have set the powers of the four quarters to cross each other.... I thus will send up a voice on behalf of everything that You have made.

Black Elk

Unknown
Oglala Lakota

Red-Armed Panther
Northen Cheyenne

INDIAN SPIRIT

All living creatures and all plants derive their life from the sun. If it were not for the sun, there would be darkness and nothing could grow—the earth would be without life. Yet the sun must have the help of the earth. If the sun alone were to act upon animals and plants, the heat would be so great that they would die, but there are clouds that bring rain, and the action of the sun and earth together supply the moisture that is needed for life…. This is according to the laws of nature and is one of the evidences of the wisdom of <u>Wakan</u> <u>Tanka</u>….

The reason <u>Wakan</u> <u>Tanka</u> does not make two birds, or animals, or human beings exactly alike is because each is placed here by <u>Wakan</u> <u>Tanka</u> to be an independent individuality and to rely on itself. Some animals are made to live in the ground. The stones and the minerals are placed in the ground by <u>Wakan</u> <u>Tanka</u>, some stones being more exposed than others. When a medicine man says that he talks with the sacred stones, it is because of all the substances in the ground these are the ones which most often appear in dreams and are able to communicate with men. A man ought to desire that which is genuine instead of that which is artificial.

Shooter
Lakota

Whenever there is any trouble,
I shall not die but get through.
Though arrows are many,
I shall arrive.
My heart is manly.

Plains Indian war song

When I was ten years of age I looked at the land and the rivers, the sky above, and the animals around me and could not fail to realize that they were made by some great power. I was so anxious to understand this power that I questioned the trees and the bushes. It seemed as though the flowers were staring at me, and I wanted to ask them, "Who made you?" I looked at the moss-covered stones; some of them seemed to have the features of a man, but they could not answer me. Then I had a dream, and in my dream one of these small round stones appeared to me and told me that the maker of all was <u>Wakan Tanka</u>, and that in order to honor Him I must honor His works in nature.

Brave Buffalo
Hunkpapa Lakota

You ask me to plow the ground. Shall I take a knife and tear my mother's breast? Then when I die she will not take me to her bosom to rest.

You ask me to dig for stone. Shall I dig under her skin for bones? Then when I die I cannot enter her body to be born again.

You ask me to cut grass and make hay and sell it, and be rich like white men. But how dare I cut off my mother's hair?

It is a bad law, and my people cannot obey it. I want my people to stay with me here. All the dead men will come to life again. We must wait here in the house of our fathers and be ready to meet them in the body of our mother.

Smohalla, Nez Perce

Crazy Thunder
Oglala Lakota

*It does not require many words
to speak the truth.*

Rolling Thunder
(Chief Joseph)
Nez Perce

As a Nez Perce man passed through the forest the moving trees whispered to him and his heart swelled with the song of the swaying pine. He looked through the green branches and saw white clouds drifting across the blue dome, and he felt the song of the clouds. Each bird twittering in the branches, each water-fowl among the reeds or on the surface of the lake, spoke its intelligible message to his heart; and as he looked into the sky and saw the high-flying birds of passage, he knew that their flight was made strong by the uplifted voices of ten thousand birds of the meadow, forest, and lake, and his heart, fairly in tune with all this, vibrated with the songs of its fullness. Indians with a simple system in which the individual possessed only the spirit of the bird or the beast revealed to him are indeed close to nature, but the individual Nez Perce, with his interwoven devotional system, communed with almost unlimited nature.

Rolling Thunder (Chief Joseph)

Touch the Clouds
Southern Cheyenne

Wolf Plume
Piegan Blackfeet

INDIAN SPIRIT

Iroquois Constitution:
Do not abuse your wife. If you make your wife suffer, you will die in a short time. Our grandmother, the earth, is a woman, and in mistreating your wife, you are abusing her. Most certainly will you be abusing our grandmother if you act thus. Since it is she who takes care of us, by your action you will be practically killing yourself.

Never do anything wrong to your children. Whatever your children ask you to do, do it for them. If you act in this manner people will say that you are good-natured.

Now if you do all that I have told you, you lead a happy and prosperous life. It is for that reason that when the Indians have a child whom they love they preach to him, so that he would never become acquainted with the things that are not right and never do anything wrong. Then if in later life a person did anything wrong, he would do it with a clear knowledge of the consequences of his action. This is all.

A Winnebago Father's Teachings to His Son

The feathered and blanketed figure of the American Indian has come to symbolize the American continent. He is the man who through centuries has been molded and sculpted by the same hand that shaped its mountains, forests, and plains, and marked the course of its rivers.

The American Indian is of the soil, whether it be the region of forests, plains, pueblos, or mesas. He fits into the landscape, for the hand that fashioned the continent also fashioned the man for his surroundings. He once grew as naturally as the wild sunflowers; he belongs just as the buffalo belonged.

With a physique that fitted, the man developed fitting skills—crafts which today are called American. And the body had a soul, also formed and molded by the same master hand of harmony. Out of the Indian approach to existence there came a great freedom—an intense and absorbing love for nature; a respect for life; enriching faith in a Supreme Power; and principles of truth, honesty, generosity, equity, and brotherhood.

Standing Bear, Oglala Lakota

Long Bear
Oglala Lakota

INDIAN SPIRIT

Trouble no man about his religion—respect him in his view of the Great Spirit, and demand of him that he respect yours. Treat with respect such things as he holds sacred. Do not force your religion on anyone.

Wabasha and Red Jacket, Seneca

The Great Spirit will not punish us for what we do not know. He will do justice to his red children. These black coats (missionaries) talk to the Great Spirit, and ask for light that we may see as they do, when they are blind themselves and quarrel about the light that guides them. These things we do not understand, and the light which they give us makes the straight and plain path trod by our fathers, dark and dreary.... We are few and weak, but may for a long time be happy if we hold fast to our country, and the religion of our fathers.

Red Jacket

INDIAN SPIRIT

I was born in Nature's wide domain! The trees were all that sheltered my infant limbs, the blue heavens all that covered me. I am one of Nature's children. I have always admired her. She shall be my glory: her features, her robes, and the wreath about her brow, the seasons, her stately oaks, and the evergreen—her hair, ringlets over the earth—all contribute to my enduring love of her.

And wherever I see her, emotions of pleasure roll in my breast, and swell and burst like waves on the shores of the ocean, in prayer and praise to Him who has placed me in her hand. It is thought great to be born in palaces, surrounded with wealth but to be born in Nature's wide domain is greater still!

I would much more glory in this birthplace, with the broad canopy of heaven above me, and the giant arms of the forest trees for my shelter, than to be born in palaces of marble, studded with pillars of gold! Nature will be Nature still, while palaces shall decay and fall in ruins.

Yes, Niagara will be Niagara a thousand years hence! The rainbow, a wreath over her brow, shall continue as long as the sun, and the flowing of the river—while the work of art, however carefully protected and preserved, shall fade and crumble into dust!

Kahgegagahbowh, Ojibwa

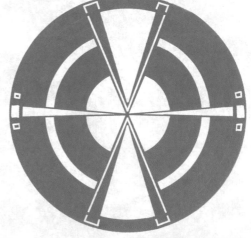

Iron Shell
Brule Lakota

White Frog
Northern Cheyenne

I do not always ask, in my prayers and discussions, for only those things I would like to see happen, because no man can claim to know what is best for mankind. Wakan Tanka and Grandfather alone know what is best, and this is why, even though I am worried, my attitude is not overcome with fear of the future. I submit always to Wakan Tanka's will. This is not easy, and most people find it impossible. But I have seen the power of prayer and I have seen God's desires fulfilled. So I pray always that God will give me the wisdom to accept His ways of doing things.

Fools Crow, Oglala Lakota

I decided to go again to Bear Butte to fast and pray ... and do you know what happened? Wakan Tanka and Tunkashila gave me the same answer I was given on my trip there in 1927. The Sioux should go back and pick up the good things that our grandfathers, grandmothers, aunts, uncles, fathers, and mothers had taught us. Our only hope was to fall back upon our traditional way of life. It was the only foundation we had that would give meaning and purpose to us. I brought this message back to the elders.

Fools Crow

INDIAN SPIRIT

Oh, yes, I went to the white man's schools. I learned to read from schoolbooks, newspapers, and the Bible. But in time I found that these were not enough. Civilized people depend too much on man-made printed pages. I turn to the Great Spirit's book, which is the whole of His creation. You can read a big part of that book if you study nature. You know, if you take all your books, lay them out under the sun, and let the snow and rain and insects work on them for a while, there will be nothing left. But the Great Spirit has provided you and me with an opportunity for study in nature's university, the forests, the rivers, the mountains, and the animals, which include us.

Walking Buffalo, Stoney

In my opinion, it was chiefly owing to their deep contemplation in their silent retreats in the days of youth that the old Indian orators acquired the habit of carefully arranging their thoughts.

They listened to the warbling of birds and noted the grandeur and the beauties of the forest. The majestic clouds—which appear like mountains of granite floating in the air—the golden tints of a summer evening sky, and all the changes of nature, possessed a mysterious significance.

All this combined to furnish ample matter for reflection to the contemplating youth.

Blackbird, Ottawa

Conquering Bear
Oglala Lakota

Scabby Bull
Arapaho

When a Lakota does anything in a formal manner he should first smoke the pipe. This is because the spirit in the pipe smoke is pleasing to <u>Wakan</u> <u>Tanka</u> and to all spirits. In any ceremony this should be the first thing that is done. To do this right the smoking material should be carefully prepared and mixed. If one is to smoke for another ceremony, he should sing a song or pray to a God while preparing the smoking material.... A man may smoke alone, and if he is doing so as a ceremony he should smoke the pipe until its contents are all consumed and then he should empty the ashes into the fire so that all may be consumed. This is because if the contents of a pipe that is smoked as a ceremony are emptied on the ground someone may step on them, or spit on them, and this would make <u>Wakan</u> <u>Tanka</u> angry. But if more than one is to smoke they do so because the spirit in the pipe will make their spirits all agree. Then when the pipe is lighted it must be passed from one to another each smoking only a few whiffs, until the contents are consumed, and then the pipe should be emptied in the fire. If there is no fire burning, the contents should be emptied on the ground and carefully covered with earth.

Sword, Oglala Lakota

INDIAN SPIRIT

When it comes time to die, be not like those whose hearts are filled with the fear of death, so when their time comes they weep and pray for a little more time to live their lives over again in a different way. Sing your death song, and die like a hero going home.

Aupumut, Mohican

Washakie

I will here relate the manner in which corn first came. According to tradition, handed down to our people, a beautiful woman was seen to descend from the clouds, and alight upon the earth, by two of our ancestors, who had killed a deer and were sitting by a fire roasting a part of it to eat. They were astonished at seeing her ... and immediately went to her, taking with them a piece of the roasted venison. They presented it to her, and she ate—and told them to return to the spot where she was sitting at the end of one year, and they would find a reward for their kindness and generosity. She then ascended to the clouds, and disappeared. The two men returned to their village, and explained to the nation what they had seen, done, and heard.... When the period arrived for them to visit this consecrated ground, where they were to find a reward for their attention to the beautiful woman of the clouds, they went with a large party, and found, where her right hand had rested on the ground, corn growing—and where the left hand had rested, beans—and immediately where she had been seated, tobacco.

Black Hawk, Sauk

Washakie
Shoshone

Kicking Bear
Miniconjou Lakota

INDIAN SPIRIT

Look as they rise, rise
Over the line where sky meets the earth;
Pleiades!
Lo! They ascending, come to guide us,
Leading us safely, keeping us one;
Pleiades,
Teach us to be, like you, united.

Song to the Pleiades from the Pawnee
Hako ceremony

From <u>Wakan Tanka</u>, the Great Mystery, comes all power. It is from <u>Wakan Tanka</u> that the holy man has wisdom and the power to heal and to make holy charms. Man knows that all healing plants are given by <u>Wakan Tanka</u>; therefore are they holy. So too is the buffalo holy, because it is the gift of <u>Wakan Tanka</u>. The Great Mystery gave to men all things for their food, their clothing, and their welfare. And to man he gave also the knowledge how to use these gifts—how to find the holy healing plants, how to hunt and surround the buffalo, how to know wisdom. For all comes from <u>Wakan Tanka</u>—all.

To the holy man comes in youth the knowledge that he will be holy. The Great Mystery makes him to know this. Sometimes it is the Spirits who tell him. The Spirits come not in sleep always, but also when man is awake. When a Spirit comes it would seem as though a man stood there, but when this man has spoken and goes forth again, none may see whither he goes. Thus go the Spirits. With the Spirits the holy man may commune always, and they teach him holy things.

The holy man goes apart to a lone tipi and fasts and prays. Or he goes into the hills in solitude. When he returns to men, he teaches them and tells them what the Great Mystery has bidden him to tell. He counsels, he heals, and he makes holy charms to protect the people from all evil. Great is his power and greatly is he revered; his place in the tipi is an honored one.

Maza Blaska (Flat-Iron), Lakota

The real character of peoples is never fully known until there has been obtained some knowledge of their religious ideas and their conception of the Unseen Power that animates all life. It is not generally credited by the white race that the tribes of this continent did not differ from the other people of the earth, in the effort to understand the meaning of life in all its infinite variety of forms and the relation of these forms to the great, mysterious Power that animates all life. It is true, however, that the natives of this land had given these themes much thought and had formulated their ideas concerning them long before the European set foot upon this soil.... Man is a religious being. Wherever he has been discovered upon the face of the earth, in whatever climate or in whatever condition, he has been found to have a religion, based upon some conception of a Power that brought into existence all things and put into them life and motion.... The true religious ideas of the Indian will never be fully comprehended, for already many of the rites and ceremonies that kept alive such conceptions as we have been considering are being forgotten in the changes that are rapidly taking place in the life of the present generation.

Francis Laflesche, Omaha

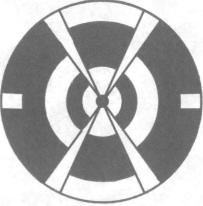

Spies on the Enemy
Absaroke

Red Wing
Absaroke

INDIAN SPIRIT

In the beginning of all things, wisdom and knowledge were with the animals, for <u>Tirawa</u>, the One Above, did not speak directly to man. He sent certain animals to tell men that He showed Himself through the beasts, and that from them, and from the stars and the sun and the moon should man learn. <u>Tirawa</u> spoke to man through His works, and the Pawnee understands the heavens, the beasts, and the plants. For all things tell of <u>Tirawa</u>.

When man sought to know how he should live, he went into solitude and cried until in vision some animal brought wisdom to him. It was <u>Tirawa</u>, in truth, who sent His message through the animal. He never spoke to man Himself, but gave His command to beast or bird, and this one came to some chosen man and taught him holy things. Thus were the sacred songs and ceremonial dances given the Pawnees through the animals.

So it was in the beginning.

In the beginning <u>Tirawa</u> gave to man the corn. The corn told man that she is mother—almighty, like <u>Tirawa</u>. If a grain of corn be split, within it will be found a juice like mother's milk. So the corn is mother, because she nourishes.

That is why, long ago, woman had all the work of planting. We might, indeed, call all women "mother." Men might call their wives "mother," for women grow the corn and cook for men; they nourish men, and give them food.

The corn is mother, but the bow and arrow is father, for the father always protects. So man must wield the bow and arrow. Thus it was long ago.

Letakots-Lesa (Eagle Chief)
Pawnee

INDIAN SPIRIT

You ought to be of some help to your fellowmen and for that reason I counsel you to fast. Our grandfather who stands in our midst [the fire] sends forth all kinds of blessings. Try then and obtain one of these. Try to have one of our grandfathers, one of the spirits, pity you. Then some day as you travel along the road of life you will know what to do and encounter no obstacles. Without any trouble you will then be able to seek the prize you desire. Then the honor will be yours to glory in, for without any exertion [by virtue of the spirit's blessings] have you obtained it. Now if you do not wear out your feet [take repeated journeys to the fasting lodge], if you do not blacken your face [with charcoal to humble yourself], it will be for naught that you inflict sufferings upon yourself. These blessings are not obtainable without effort.

Try to have one of all the spirits created by Earthmaker take pity upon you. Whatever he says will come about. If you do not possess a spirit to strengthen you, and therefore are of no consequence to the people around you, they will show you little respect. They will make fun of you.

If you tell a falsehood [about your fast] and exaggerate your account, you, in consequence, will die soon after. Those spirits who are in control of war blessings will hear you. Tell less than you did. The old men claim that it is wiser.

Such will be your life if you do what I tell you. Earthmaker created the spirits who live above the earth, those who live on the earth, those who live under the earth, and those who live in the water; all these he created and placed in charge of some powers. Even the minor spirits who move around, Earthmaker caused to have rule over some blessing. In this fashion

(continued)

White Man Runs Him
Absaroke

(continued)

He created them and only afterwards did He create us. For that reason we were not put in control of any of these blessings. However, Earthmaker did create a plant and put it in our charge, and He told us that none of the spirits He had created would have the power to take this away from us without giving us something in exchange. Thus said Earthmaker. Even He, Earthmaker, would not have the power of taking this from us without giving up something in return. He told us that if we offered Him a pipeful of tobacco, if this we poured out for Him, He would grant us whatever we asked of Him. Now all the spirits came to long for this tobacco as intensely as they longed for anything in creation, and for that reason, if at any time we make our cry to the spirits with tobacco, they will take pity on us and bestow on us the blessings of which Earthmaker placed them in charge. Indeed so it shall be, for thus Earthmaker created it.

A Winnebago
Father's Teachings to
His Son

Hollow Horn Bear, Brule Lakota, at an unknown gathering with unidentified Lakotas

INDIAN SPIRIT

You are my husband/ wife
My feet shall run because of you,
My feet, dance because of you,
My eyes, see because of you,
My mind, think because of you,
And I shall love because of you.

Eskimo wedding vow

Now we feel no rain, for each of us will be shelter to the
    other,
Now we will feel no cold, for each of us will be warmth to
    the other.
Now there is no loneliness for us,
Now we are two bodies, but only one life.
We go now to our dwelling place, to enter into the days of
    our togetherness.
May our days be good and long upon this earth.

Apache wedding prayer

Cry of the Wolf
Kiowa

INDIAN SPIRIT

Long ago the Great Mystery caused this land to be, and made the Indians to live in this land. Well has the Indian fulfilled all the intent of the Great Mystery for him. Men should know that the Indian people were made by the Great Mystery for a purpose.

Once, only Indians lived in this land. Then came strangers from across the Great Water. No land had they; we gave them of our land. No food had they; we gave them of our corn. The strangers are become many and they fill all the country. They dig gold—from my mountains; they build houses—of the trees of my forests; they rear cities—of my stones and rocks; they make fine garments—from the hides and wool of animals that eat my grass. None of the things that make their riches did they bring with them from beyond the Great Water; all comes from my land, the land the Great Mystery gave unto the Indian.

And when I think upon this I know that it is right, even thus. In the heart of the Great Mystery it was meant that stranger-visitors—my friends across the Great Water—should come to my land; that I should bid them welcome; that all men should sit down with me and eat together of my corn. It was meant by the Great Mystery that the Indian should give to all peoples.

But the white man never has known the Indian. It is thus: there are two roads, the white man's road, and the Indian's road. Neither traveler knows the road of the other. Thus ever has it been, from the long ago, even unto today.

I want all Indians and white men to read and learn how the Indians lived and thought in the olden time, and may it bring holy-good upon the younger Indians to know of their fathers. A little while, and the old Indians will no longer be, and the young will be even as white men. When I think, I know that it is the mind of the Great Mystery that white men and Indians who fought together should now be one people.

There are birds of many colors—red, blue, green, yellow—yet it is all one bird. There are horses of many colors—brown, black, yellow, white—yet it is all one horse. So cattle, so all living things—animals, flowers, trees. So men: in this land where once were only Indians are now men of every color—white, black, yellow, red—yet all one people. That this should come to pass was in the heart of the Great Mystery. And everywhere there shall be peace.

Hiamovi (High Chief), Cheyenne

Comes Out Holy
Oglala Lakota

Oh! that I could make that of my Red people, and of my country, as great as the conceptions of my mind, when I think of the Spirit that rules the universe.

Tecumseh (Shooting Star), Shawnee

Index of Photographs

Index of Quotations

Index of Photographers

Primary Bibliography

There are many sources for the older quotations of the great chiefs, most of which are no longer in print. The following books remain in print and are sources for many of the quotations used in this book. All of these books are recommended reading.

Brown, Joseph E., *The Sacred Pipe: Black Elk's Account of the Seven Rites of the Oglala Sioux.* Norman: University of Oklahoma, 1971.

DeMallie, Raymond J., *The Sixth Grandfather: Black Elk's Teachings Given to John G. Neihardt.* Lincoln: University of Nebraska Press, 1984.

Fitzgerald, Michael O., *Yellowtail: Crow Medicine Man and Sun Dance Chief.* Norman: University of Oklahoma Press, 1991.

Fitzgerald, Michael O., *Light on the Indian World: The Essential Writings of Charles Eastman (Ohiyesa).* Bloomington: World Wisdom, 2002.

Jackson, Donald, *Black Hawk: An Autobiography.* Urbana and Chicago: University of Illinois Press, 1964.

Mails, Thomas E., *Fools Crow.* Garden City: Doubleday, 1979.

Neihardt, John G., *Black Elk Speaks.* Lincoln: University of Nebraska Press, 1961.

Schuon, Frithjof, *The Feathered Sun.* Bloomington: World Wisdom Books, 1990.

Standing Bear, Luther, *Land of the Spotted Eagle.* Lincoln: University of Nebraska Press, 1980.

Standing Bear, Luther, *My People the Sioux.* Lincoln: University of Nebraska Press, 1975.

Vanderwerth, W.C., *Indian Oratory: Famous Speeches by Noted Indian Chieftains.* Norman: University of Oklahoma Press, 1979.

Walker, James R., *Lakota Belief and Ritual.* Edited by Raymond J. DeMallie and Elaine A. Jahner. Lincoln: University of Nebraska Press, 1980.

Walker, James R., *Lakota Myth.* Edited by Elaine A. Jahner. Lincoln: University of Nebraska Press, 1989.

Biographical Notes

Judith and Michael Fitzgerald have spent extended periods of time visiting traditional cultures and attending sacred ceremonies throughout the world, including the sacred rites of the Apsaroke, Sioux, Cheyenne, Shoshone, Bannock, and Apache tribes. The Fitzgeralds have collaborated on a series of successful inspirational quote books, including *The Spirit of Indian Women* (World Wisdom, 2006) and *Christian Spirit*, which won the award for the best book in Religion and Philosophy in 2004 by the Midwest Independent Publisher's Association. Both Michael and Judith have been adopted into the Apsaroke tribe and the family of the late Thomas Yellowtail, one of the most honored American Indian spiritual leaders of the last century. They are married, have an adult son, and live in Bloomington, Indiana.

Michael Oren Fitzgerald has written and edited numerous publications on world religions, particularly on American Indian spirituality. Four of his books on American Indian spirituality are used in college courses. He holds a Doctor of Jurisprudence, cum laude, from Indiana University. Michael has taught Religious Traditions of the North American Indians in the Indiana University Continuing Studies Department in Bloomington, Indiana. Judith Fitzgerald is a graduate of Indiana University. She is an artisan, calligrapher, and graphic designer.

What Others Have Said:

"One of the great callings of art is to excavate a lost part of our culture, and the Fitzgeralds answer this summons handsomely here in a compact exploration of Native American women's spirituality."

—Publishers Weekly on *The Spirit of Indian Women*

"*The Spirit of Indian Women* … is an act of reclamation as much as of spirituality: it reproduces precious and seldom-seen photographs of Native American women, most of them from the later 19th century. Their images are interwoven with oral accounts, songs, and other documents that offer priceless glimpses into the little-understood lives and experiences of America's foremothers…. *The Spirit of Indian Women* is a special treasure. Highly recomended."

—Library Journal

"*The Sermon of All Creation* is founded on the very ancient and venerable Christian tradition of insight drawn from 'God's second Book.' Dazzling photographs, saturated with color, share pages with quotations from the likes of Catherine of Siena, Augustine of Hippo, and William Penn; the volume includes an index of authors for easy reference."

—Library Journal

"Michael Fitzgerald has heard the poignant narratives of the American Indian people, and has lived among the Crow people for extended periods of time since 1970. He has studied American Indian religious traditions on the earth, among the people, in ceremonies and family gatherings. We thank Fitzgerald for his deep-seated appreciation, honor, and respect for American Indian culture, its religion, language, and lifeways."

—Janine Pease, founding president of the Little Big Horn College, and National Indian Educator of the Year

"My son, Michael Fitzgerald, has been a member of my family and the Crow tribe for over twenty years. Michael has helped to preserve the spiritual traditions of the Crow Sun Dance and he has helped to show us the wisdom of the old-timers."

—Thomas Yellowtail, Crow Medicine Man and Sun Dance Chief

"I greatly appreciate the recovery work that Fitzgerald is doing, work that makes available for the classroom and popular use texts that have been all but buried in libraries. Work such as Fitzgerald's is exactly the kind of work that needs to be promoted for a more complete understanding of early American Indian writings and oratory."

—Stephen Brandon, University of New Mexico

Other Books by Judith and Michael Oren Fitzgerald

Christian Spirit, World Wisdom, 2004
{Awarded best book on "Religion and Philosophy—2004" by MIPA}

The Sermon of All Creation: Christians on Nature, World Wisdom, 2005

The Spirit of Indian Women, World Wisdom, 2005
{Awarded best book on "Religion and Philosophy—2005" by MIPA}

The Universal Spirit of Islam, World Wisdom 2006

The Spirit of Muhammad: From Hadith, World Wisdom, 2008

Other Books by Michael Oren Fitzgerald

Yellowtail: Crow Medicine Man and Sun Dance Chief,
University of Oklahoma Press, 1991

Light on the Indian World: The Essential Writings of Charles Eastman (Ohiyesa),
World Wisdom, 2002

Indian Spirit, World Wisdom, 2003

The Foundations of Christian Art: Illustrated, by Titus Burckhardt,
World Wisdom, 2006

Native Spirit: The Sun Dance Way, World Wisdom, 2007

Introduction to Hindu Dharma: Discourses by the 68th Jagadguru of Kanchipuram, World Wisdom, 2008

Films Produced by Michael Oren Fitzgerald

Native Spirit: The Sun Dance Way, World Wisdom, 2007
{Selected for the "First Peoples' Festival—PRÉSENCE AUTOCHTONE" in Montreal}

About James Trosper

James Trosper is a Sun Dance Chief of the Shoshone Tribe on the Wind River Indian Reservation in Wyoming. He is from a long line of Shoshone Sun Dance chiefs and is a direct descendent of Chief Washakie, who is the most important chief of the Shoshone tribe in history (see photographs on pp. 122-123). Mr. Trosper is deeply involved in developing and promoting programs to preserve the Shoshone language and cultural heritage. He is also part Arapaho, a director of the Chief Washakie Foundation, and a Trustee of the University of Wyoming.

Film interviews with James Trosper on Shoshone spirituality, tribal history, and advice for American Indian youth are a featured part of the documentary film and DVD on the Crow Shoshone Sun Dance entitled *Native Spirit: The Sun Dance Way*. The interviews are transcribed and included in a companion book also entitled *Native Spirit: The Sun Dance Way*. Both the film and the book are published by World Wisdom, 2007.

James Trosper, his wife, and their two children, live in Fort Washakie, WY.

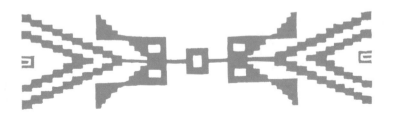

About Thomas Yellowtail

Born in 1903, medicine man and Sun Dance chief Thomas Yellowtail was the principal figure in the Crow-Shoshone Sun Dance Religion during the last half of the 20th century. As a youth he lived in the presence of old warriors, hunters, and medicine men who knew the freedom and sacred ways of pre-reservation life. In February 1993, when Yellowtail received the Montana Governor's Award for the Arts, in recognition of his work in preserving the traditional culture of the Crow tribe, the program for the award ceremony contained the following quotation:

> This man is outside of time as we know it, centered in the spiritual world. Thomas Yellowtail has perpetuated the spiritual traditions of his Crow tribe as one of the last living links to pre-reservation days. But his legacy is not limited to Native Americans because his principles and his message benefit anyone searching to find a balance in this fast-paced technological society.

Yellowtail died at age 90 in 1993. He was one of the most admired American Indian spiritual leaders of the last century, although he was not the most prominent member of his immediate family. Historically, the Yellowtail family is the most famous Crow family of the 20th century. His older brother, Robert Yellowtail, was the first Native American superintendent of a reservation and was selected as Commissioner of Indian Affairs by President Eisenhower, although he declined the appointment. Yellowtail Dam and Yellowtail Reservoir in Montana are named after him. Susie Yellowtail, Thomas Yellowtail's wife, was the first Native American registered nurse, a tireless advocate of Native American issues and is already enshrined in the Montana Hall of Fame in Helena, Montana. The many honors and awards that have been received by the Yellowtail family, including Thomas Yellowtail, are too numerous to mention. The story of his life and his descriptions of the Sun Dance Religion are revealed in the book *Yellowtail: Crow Medicine Man and Sun Dance Chief*, edited by Michael Fitzgerald. It was published by the University of Oklahoma Press (1991).

A documentary film and DVD about the Crow-Shoshone Sun Dance entitled *Native Spirit: The Sun Dance Way* contains film and photographs of more than twenty Crow and Shoshone Sun Dances and is based upon the Yellowtail autobiography. The DVD contains extensive film interviews with Thomas Yellowtail and is also available as an illustrated book.

About *Yellowtail: Crow Medicine Man & Sun Dance Chief*

"As (Yellowtail) recounts his extraordinary personal experiences and defines the Crow religion, the magnitude of the loss to his people emerges along with wonder at his enduring faith and strength of spirit.... A book of wisdom that contributes mightily to the study of religion and Native American life.... Important material for students investigating native American history, anthropology, or religions."

—Booklist Magazine

"(Fitzgerald's) book becomes the personal testament of a pivotal figure in recent Crow cultural history. The book describes in exquisite detail Yellowtail's philosophy. Fitzgerald examines the place of the Sun Dance, and of the sacred, in the life and future of the Crow.... It is a serious work of anthropology and history."

—Choice Magazine

"This new window onto the remarkable world of the Native American may be among the last that will be opened to us, for Yellowtail is one of the few remaining living links to that irreplaceable past. What is important is that this latest window is also one of our best.... The result is a compelling testament that may come in time to rival *Black Elk Speaks*."

—Huston Smith, University of California, Berkeley

"Authentic and conveying the character of Yellowtail's voice."

—Publishers Weekly

Free American Indian e-Products

Daily Inspirational Quotations

Judith and Michael Fitzgerald have also selected many American Indian inspirational quotations and designed and created many patterns of American Indian e-stationery for use on the Internet. The quotations and e-stationery are combined to create "daily inspirational American Indian quotations" that can be automatically sent to readers each day via e-mail at no charge. Interested readers should visit the e-Products section of the publisher's Internet site at:

www.worldwisdom.com

Other Free e-Products

Judith Fitzgerald has also created American Indian wallpaper, screen savers, e-cards, and e-stationery that are available for no cost at the same website. New products are periodically added. World Wisdom provides all of these products to readers at no cost. The publisher and the editors hope these products will also provide a source of daily inspiration.